RAMBLINGS

of a

Right Wing
Bible Thumping
White Guy!

Joe Messina

Political Illustrations by A.F. Branco   www.comicallyincorrect.com

Ramblings of a Right Wing, Bible Thumping, White Guy

Copyright © 2016 Joe Messina

ISBN-13: 978-1539717379

ISBN-10: 1539717372

Dedication

I could make a lot of people happy by simply placing what some would believe to be the "correct and obvious" names here. BUT I never do the politically correct thing.

This book is properly dedicated to:
Vincent James Mercadante
"Big Bill" or Uncle Bill to me.

Uncle Bill was like my second father. Like in most big families, and mine being Italian, I spent many days, weekends, and summers with my cousins and my Uncle and Aunt.

Uncle Bill served his country in the Army and then came home and again defended us by becoming a Boston policeman. He was a founding member of the Boston Police Patrolmen's Association.

He was always very black and white. I used to listen to him when he talked to his buddies and other family members and he never left any wiggle room for stupidity or foolishness (always in love). When I got older, I both hated and appreciated his ability to draw attention to your shortcomings through sarcasm. Uncle would never accept uninformed excuses and reasons. You better have the truth, facts, and proof before dealing with him. Always fair and always helpful!

Uncle Bill passed away in 2011 and continues to be VERY much missed. I'm a very blessed person for having had him in my life.

Foreword

Remember that iconic movie scene when Col. Nathan Jessop, played by Jack Nicholson, screamed **"YOU CAN'T HANDLE THE TRUTH"** from the witness stand in A Few Good Men?

Well, we're about to find out if you (yea, the one holding this book right now) can handle the truth. Because Joe Messina is about to fire truth at you faster than my BushMaster AR-15 can empty a 30 round magazine of .223 rounds.

Joe's Boston raised penchant for just telling it like it is has still not been tempered by his years living in the people's republic of California. And thank the good Lord for it! Every reader of this book will greatly benefit by the absolute absence of political correctness.

If you'd like the straight truth, however hard it may be to take, about just how far off the rails we've let our nation slide... this book is for you!

Prepare to be offended, infuriated, awakened, motivated, and encouraged to actually do something about the insanity!

Rick Green *is Host of "WallBuilders Live w/David Barton" and co-star of "Chasing American Legends." For more information, visit www.RickGreen.com*

Table of Contents

INTRODUCTION

I am neither a book reader, nor a book writer... until today. And we'll have to see how this one turns out. It is now my 8th year in radio, doing a daily weekday show. What started out as pure politics eventually morphed into all kinds of social and other ridiculous issues that are almost never heard about on mainstream media.

My first socially foul story was about "mommy and me pole dancing classes" in Northern California. I couldn't believe it was true. But it was. Then there was the Nebraska school district that decided children in elementary school would no longer be called girls and boys, but purple penguins. Because, you know, they were gender-neutral and socially acceptable in every way! Then we had "trigger word" protection on college campuses and "safe rooms." The flushing sound just got louder and louder as the years went on. Crazy has become the new norm in America.

At first I thought it was just me. It had to be my "white privilege." I couldn't understand why we needed 27 different pronouns and gender identifiers for people. So I started sending these stories and thoughts to my friend and professional "shrink," Dr. Michelle Skeen out of San Francisco. I got a clean bill of health (for now!)

Since white privilege is such a big issue I pondered about how my white privilege had helped me out through the years. I grew up in a very poor section of Boston, called the North End. It may be hard to believe, but I had no idea we were poor. I was loved. My backyard was the rooftop of the building next door. My front yard was usually filled with cars and I had to wait for them to clear out before I could play in it. Yes, it was the street In front of our apartment. I lived at 4 Henchman Street (go ahead and Google it) in Boston. It's only blocks from the Old North Church and about 10 blocks from Paul Revere's house. In the late 1960's to early 1970's it was said this section was as congested with people as Bangladesh. That was my white privilege at work.

INTRODUCTION

There wasn't a lot of money for anything in spite of my white privilege. My mom worked pretty hard to support us. There were no supermarkets where we lived. We had butchers, bakers, and mini grocery stores, just like you see in the movies. We walked up metal stairs to the apartment with grocery bags. That was my white privilege.

When my mom was able to move me out to a better area, there were not many other Italians. I often heard words I was unfamiliar with; "Dago," "Guinea," "Greaseball," and "Wop" (and some I can't print without making the book R-rated.) Most were used by my "WASP" friends (White Anglo -Saxon Protestant) who didn't consider me "white." I was a man without a color designation!

When asked about all these new designations, my Uncle Eddie's response was, "They're idiots. You can't fight with ignorant idiots." At some point, I figured he was right and I just let it go. But as you can see, I wasn't treated with that "white privilege" I hear talked about so much.

I worked hard to get my first job, apartment, and car. I had black, Jewish, Asian, and, yes, even Irish friends. We all saw ourselves as equals. We cared for each other and fought for each other. *WHAT THE HECK HAS HAPPENED?!?*

A regular on my show, and a covert to the truth of these stories, said, "Gee Joe, after 7 years of this you have MORE than enough to write a book." Thought she was nuts. Then my publicist said, "Joe, you're coming up on 8 years and it's an election year. What are you waiting for?"

No more waiting. After 8 years and hundreds of stories, I've decided to put together the most egregious stories. You may have a hard time believing they're real. Trust me, they are.

Keep a barf bag close by and strap in for the ride!

Chapter 1

Absolutes? Absolutely NOT!

News cycles are dictated by so-called "news sources." They put out, and repeatedly harp on, what they believe is most important for society to know about but they couldn't care less what society really thinks is important.

Technology is one of the hard Left's biggest fears. It leaves a residue... a record of speeches that should only be heard by certain groups, statistics of long ago (climate change, cooling, warming), and comments like "what difference does it make?" "I did not have sexual relations with that woman," and the most memorable, "if you like your doctor, you can keep your doctor." Until he was caught, and then he said, "Let me be clear" (yeah right!) "I said if you like your doctor AND he is part of the plan, you can keep your doctor." With flip-flopping, wordsmithing, and backtracking like that, I have to ask, are there ANY absolutes?

I'm a homophobe if I don't agree that the gay and lesbian lifestyle is OK. I move to hater status if I take it to the next level with, "I don't agree with same sex marriage."

And I'm a racist if I don't agree with just about anything else the Left says I should like, accept, and approve of!

The words racist, homophobe, and hater all have a specific meaning and, according to years and years of definition, are to be applied to very specific situations. It used to be, if you were labeled with one of those words, you needed to check yourself! They have now become a simple bullying tool for the Left to get the weak-spined, thin-skinned conservatives to bow to their wishes.

Remember, strength comes when you bow only to truth!

In our world, we now teach our kids that there are no more boys and girls. Gender neutrality is good because it gives you time to figure out what gender you want to be when you get older. Oh, and you can CHANGE it any time you feel like! I'm sure that doesn't cause any confusion at all!

Colleges are now asking that you not call each other Miss or Sir, young lady, or young man. But they also haven't really given any clear direction as to what to call them or how to know what to call them. Is there a marker, a bandana, a wrist band, or t-shirt perhaps? More no definitive lines.

You can choose your own gender (and anything in between.) Bruce/Caitlyn Jenner is almost there, but not quite. He still has male parts... and now some female parts. His face and upper half has been redone to the tune of $72,000 and he wants to be called a "she" because he feels like a she. If his body (God forbid,

and I wish no ill on this person) was found charred beyond recognition in the remains of a house fire, DNA, the life source by which your body functions and grows, would definitely show him  to be a man. But we are told science doesn't matter when it comes to gender, only one's feelings and thoughts are real!

If Rachel Dolezal, the black, no wait the white girl (who chose to be black), was found (God forbid, and I wish no ill on this person either) charred beyond recognition in the remains of a house fire, DNA, the life source by which your body functions and grows, would definitely show her to be a Caucasian. But because she feels black, or identifies with the black community, she is allowed to call herself black with very little outcry from the Left! I wonder what her Party affiliation is?

RAMBLINGS

And, as if that weren't enough, the right Rev. Al Sharpton came out and questioned her parents' motives. Let me help you Al. If she took a gun into NAACP headquarters and shot a bunch of black people, you'd be asking for tighter gun control, for her to be charged with a hate crime because a white person shot black people, and you'd be asking why her parents never spoke up about the fact that she had a lying problem and that she might have some issues "between the ears." Al, is it wrong to lie or not? The Bible says it is! What say you, Reverend?

Guns kill people. YEP! And birds and rattlesnakes and alligators and lions and bears and a multitude of other animals. Talk about a foggy argument. How many people have been intentionally killed for no reason by law-abiding, sane citizens who legally carry? Anybody? NONE! That's right NONE!

The president's unsubstantiated (as usual) claim that we have more violent killings than other developed countries is just a lie, plain and simple. And there's still no real talk about mental health. No real talk about the dangers of bringing up our children without clear boundaries of right and wrong.

The people who have this 100% right are the people at the Charleston AME church. They called for no riots. They wanted prayer. No hatred. Just love. They stood for the real, solid truth. The only truth that can free us all and get us out of the foggy and twisted thinking we have allowed to creep into society and take over. The truth that comes from the Word of God. The trust, as you may have heard many in the church say, which comes from Jesus Christ.

The government and the loons tell you, there is no wrong or right. If it feels right, it's right for you. You don't need to sacrifice at all... ever! If you have all the equipment of a male but feel like a female, that doesn't matter. You can change it! If you feel like a female and you want to be a male then change it! If you are born to a white family and you want to be identified as black, no problem! Lie on your applications and writings and change it.

There was an immediate outcry for the white maniac that killed 9 people at the Charleston AME Church to be labeled a terrorist and categorized as a hate crime. Yet there was relative silence on the Fort Hood massacre labeling it a work-related crime. The first had mental illness and drugs attached to it. The second was pure hate for non-Muslims. Both have pure evil attached. Is there an absolute?

Mr. President, HELP! What constitutes a hate crime? When is it racial or religious? What do you actually mean by tougher gun laws? If congress hasn't come through, why don't you submit a plan to them... and NOT by Executive Order!

~ ~

People, your kids are confused and it's easy to see why. Black is not black. White is a schism and hateful. Boys aren't, and neither are girls.

~ ~

People, your kids are confused and it's easy to see why. Black is not black. White is a schism and hateful. Boys aren't, and neither are girls. You work hard but you're really doing nothing because you can't "build that on your own" according to President Obama. What a confusing world for our children to have to find their way in.

I guess now I know what my mom meant when she said, "you can grow up and be anything you want to be." Boy, did she call that one right!

Chapter 2

The LEFT needs Racism

When all the garbage was going on in Baltimore after Freddie Gray's death while in police custody, we saw something we don't see very often... a parent take control of her teenage child who was going to where the riots were happening. Once the vandalism started it changed from protests to riots. But that mom marched through the crowd not caring about her own safety in order to save her child's life. God bless this woman! But the left curses her!

The left doesn't see this women as a real hero doing something that we don't see much of today... a parent saying "no, no way, not my child, not today." She said she wasn't going to allow her son to disrespect property, disrespect the police, and destroy the community. She said he promised her he would not go down there! So, as SHE said, he lied and went where he should not have been.

This single mom with 6 children took time off from work to be involved. She said when she saw him with his face covered and a brick in his hand she knew he was up to no good. She grabbed him and started smacking him around (with an OPEN hand.) She told him if he wanted to protest he should be a man, show his face, and do it the right way... using nonviolence. (Remember, all you who love Dr. Martin Luther King Jr.'s nonviolence?)

She did a good thing. She held her son accountable for his actions!

But did she really? The loons on the Left say "no"! They say what she did was the wrong way. Baltimore child protective services was asked to investigate. Their statement, "If she would do this to her son in public, what is she doing to her kids in private?" WHAT?! Are they serious? (As of this writing the case has been closed with no charges filed.)

Let me see. We have seen many kids punch, even knock out, teachers in classroom situations or on school grounds and that's them just "acting out because of their environment." We are supposed to make excuses for them and not hold them accountable. But a mom gets physical to ensure her child does not act out criminal behavior and suddenly it's the end of the world? How has that "Time out" thing worked for us over the years?

The loons didn't like all the positive attention she was getting. In interviews, her son kept saying he knew what he was doing was wrong and didn't know his mom cared so much about what he did. WOW! A positive response from the child! We can't have that, now can we?

Then a psychologist (who happened to be black) says on CNN, that the reason this video and incident was so popular was that white people like to see black kids getting beaten up, especially a black woman beating on a black man. I call B.S... big time.

~ ~

Hey, loons! You want racism to stop? Stop making everything about race.

~ ~

Hey, loons! You want racism to stop? Stop making everything about race. You know, like the one where PB&J's are racist! Really? Is it REALLY racist that rich people can go to better schools than poor people? Or is it because there are more poor black people? And have you heard? The "war on drugs is a war on black people." Why, you ask? Because there are more black people on drugs than others. Really? Isn't that a racist comment in and of itself?

RAMBLINGS

It never crossed my mind that more blacks were on drugs than whites, Asians, and Latinos until a racist, black attorney brought it up and made my racist, white privileged self aware of the situation!

So, let's go down that road. Most stories we see on black single moms are usually about how many kids they have by how many baby-daddy's and how welfare is not giving her the money she needs to raise her children. The Right latches on and complains that we need to stop supporting this kind of behavior. The Left jumps up and says we aren't doing enough for the disadvantaged.

What's confusing is how commentators covered an uplifting story about a mom. Now understand, no conservative writer or commentator I work with used the words "black mother" until the Left made a big deal out of it. She's not on welfare. She took time off of her job to go take care of her responsibility. Yes, her 16 year-old child, who lied to her, was going down to commit felonies and possibly be injured or killed. She was mad and unashamed enough to smack him around with an open hand, and pull his face mask off to take responsibility for his actions. God bless this woman! Not this black woman teaching her black, lying son a lesson. God bless this WOMAN teaching her SON a lesson. If you used the word "black" in there, then you, sir, are the racist!

It's impossible to placate the Left. These loons want open borders, no rules, and total socialism. We can't discipline our kids or hold them responsible. We

can't expect better from them in school or work. We can't force people to work in any way, whether they be on welfare or in jail. We can't demand anything of our citizens and non-citizens, yet they can demand and expect everything from the government via the law-abiding taxpayers.

You want equality? Charge the 101 rioters and vandals let go from Baltimore holding because the system was overloaded (more B.S.) Charging 6 police officers the way they did was nothing more than appeasement, and that's wrong. Should a police officer have been charged? Maybe. But to do it and pay the family of the victim over 6 million dollars before anyone was found guilty, even before jury selection was done, is absolutely nuts! (At the time of writing this book 3 of the 6 have been acquitted and Ms. Mosby may be disbarred, go figure)

There is so much about this that stinks, but most of all, the fact that the loons want this woman demonized for striking her child in public is one of the reasons this society is falling apart!

America protect your children. Train and discipline them accordingly – and don't let the government stop you!

Chapter 3

Microaggression, Shmicroaggression

The word "microaggression" has cropped up with increased frequency over the last few years, to the point that we now see it almost daily! WTH does it mean? (*WTH means what the hell for you non hipsters*)

Webster's says it has "no meaning." It's not a word. It doesn't exist! Various blogs, papers, and online sources provide similar definitions.

And then, I found www.microaggressions.com. This site was obviously built by people who can't stand anyone who might, kinda, sorta have some type of privilege going for them. According to this site "microaggression" is defined as:

> *"Racial micro aggressions are brief and commonplace daily verbal, behavioral, or environmental indignities, whether intentional or unintentional, that communicate hostile, derogatory, or negative racial slights and insults toward people of color."*

I have said it before... words no longer have meaning and this is another perfect example of why. This definition specifically says it's aimed at people of color.

Based on the many "microaggression" stories I've covered, the definition should read as follows:

> *Micro aggressions are brief and commonplace daily verbal, behavioral, or environmental indignities, whether intentional or unintentional, that communicate hostile, derogatory, or negative slights and insults towards;* _____. (INSERT anyone identifying as LGBTQ, a woman, a minority, or some other subset of people, no matter how ridiculous.)

Microaggression, Shmicroaggression

In 2015 at Brandeis University, the Asian American Students Association was accused of a microaggression for putting up a display to explain microaggression using only Asians... REALLY?

A group at Oberlin University had to issue a warning of microaggression or triggering alerting readers they were about to see "Discussion of rape culture, online harassment, victim blaming, and rape apologism and denialism." REALLY? They needed a warning?

Johns Hopkins University refused to allow *Chick-Fil-A* to open on campus because the campus LGBTQ club considered it an act of microaggression. So now anyone or anything that offends is microaggression? Well, kinda sorta. It really only seems to apply to certain groups.

~ ~

If you ask me to remove my Bible from view, you would consider that your right not to be "assaulted" by my beliefs. But by the definitions above, wouldn't that be considered a microaggression toward me and my religion? No, silly. You can't microaggress white men or Christians.

~ ~

If you ask me to remove my Bible from view, you would consider that your right not to be "assaulted" by my beliefs. But by the definitions above, wouldn't that be considered a microaggression toward me and my religion? No, silly. You can't microaggress white men or Christians.

A recent microaggression reported at Arizona State University had students petitioning staff to change the name of pedestrian walkways. Why, you ask? Because not everyone can walk and that COULD be viewed as a microaggression to someone in a wheelchair or on crutches. Even the people who were supposed to be offended (those in wheelchairs or on crutches) thought this was ridiculous.

So what's the magic formula? Is it considered a microaggression if only one person is left out? Have we raised a group of individuals who don't know that pedestrian crossings were put in place to protect people not in a vehicle?

Since most of these microaggression dustups seem to happen on college campuses, maybe we need to add "Common Sense Definitions 101" to orientation and make it mandatory!

One of the people interviewed at Arizona State said, "I was on crutches for 5 weeks and felt uncomfortable when seeing this sign." Why? What would make this a big deal for this person? A sign made them uncomfortable. He was on crutches for a temporary period for whatever reason. Was he concerned someone would see him on crutches and he was embarrassed? Was it because he felt guilty for using the crosswalk when he was so healthy otherwise? It makes no sense. It's a crosswalk. That doesn't mean it's for people with two physically healthy legs. It means it's for non-vehicles.

This person is going to have a very hard life if a crosswalk sign caused him this much trauma!

So again I ask, what is the magic formula? Is it how many people are offended? A percentage of the whole campus or event? Does it only apply to certain groups?

Microaggression, Shmicroaggression

What about some of the curriculum that's offensive to certain religious groups? Is that a form of microaggression? Probably not. Religious people are weird, so it's OK to make fun of them and treat them differently. No problem!

Based on my research, I've concluded that microaggression is defined as:

> *A made-up word used to try to intimidate those who are too concerned about political correctness. It is aimed at non-issues that ultimately hurt no one but a few overly sensitive "humans"* (that's still an OK term, I hope) *to create a distraction away from the real issues.*

Our kids are graduating with record high debt, few prospects for jobs, and are still undereducated. Oh wait, that's probably a form of microaggression. But isn't everything?

Chapter 4

Selma march proves police are racist?

In 2015, President Obama went to Selma, Alabama to commemorate and celebrate the march across the bridge that helped bring civil rights to the forefront, into the living room of all Americans, and help move it forward. Yes, it was aimed at the black community, but as Dr. Martin Luther King, Jr. believed, all would be judged on the content of their character rather than the color of their skin... black, white, brown, or otherwise. There weren't just black people marching, white folks were also there.

I say commemorate because the people involved in the Selma march were not welcome there. They knew they could be killed. They knew they would have no place to sleep, probably not much food, and certainly not much help. They didn't care. They knew that what they were fighting for was right and, as with our forefathers, believed it was worth losing everything for, even dying for. They deserve to be remembered and honored.

This stands in stark contrast to the "protests" of today. Unlike the Black Lives Matter (BLM) people who said they were protesting unfair treatment at the hands of police, MLK's protests wanted true justice and equality, not superiority and retribution.

In Ferguson, MO, a young black man, Michael Brown, was shot to death by a police officer. One account claimed that he was shot with his hands raised in submissive surrender, and the Black Lives Matter movement was born with their rally cry, "hands up don't shoot." In the end, it turned out to be a lie. Any apologies or restoration to the policeman who had to quit and move out of town because of that LIE? No, that's not necessary, because ONLY Black Lives Matter!

These people would have made Dr. King proud, right? I am sure he would have encouraged them to loot and burn down buildings and beat up people in their communities, right? No, he would not have approved! He was for peaceful demonstrations, unlike the Reverend Al "Get-it-where-and-when-I-can" Sharpton. Rev. Al forgot that at his Millions March NYC "event." His followers chanted: "What do we want??... DEAD COPS!... When do we want them??...NOW!!!" A perfect example of Dr. King? I think not.

I say celebrate because we celebrate the sacrifices made that day in Selma by people of all colors. Yes, mostly black, but many others as well. The actions of those people that day sparked a movement that couldn't and won't be stopped!

Jump ahead 50 years. We have a black president, a black attorney general, and many positions of authority at the White House filled by people who have black skin (sorry, I'm not calling them all "African American" because I have been told by many blacks that they are not all of African descent, some are from Belize, Jamaica, and so on.) We have come a long way in 50 years. Are we perfect? No. I believe the Bible says let the one without sin cast the first stone. But we are still the best country to be living in on this planet. Yes, I believe in American exceptionalism. Even with our faults, people still have more opportunity here than any other country.

I have to first say, the president made many good and honest remarks in his speech about the sacrifices made in Selma that day for black Americans. But it stops there.

He then went down the political rabbit trail. He mentioned Ferguson. Not to say that anyone was wrong and jumped to conclusions with "hands up don't shoot!" No. He talked about the findings report saying,

"The Justice Department's report on the Ferguson, MO police department shows that not enough has changed in the country with respect to race relations."

RAMBLINGS

~ ~

Really? He used the report from one police department and applied it to all police departments across the whole country? Really?

~ ~

Really? He used the report from one police department and applied it to all police departments across the whole country? Really?

Look at the stats. Race relations in this country were on the mend and getting MUCH better until around, let me think, 2009. Do your own homework!

The DOJ, run at the time by his buddy Eric Holder, said there was no crime committed by the police officer in this incident. How much time did mainstream media give to that? Not much at all. Where are the leaders in the black community speaking to the issue of the truth of what really took place in Ferguson? Nowhere to be found.

It's interesting how the leader of the Democrat party, President Obama, the Party that wanted to pull God out of their platform, seemed to have no problem invoking and reading scripture from the Bible. OMG! Where are the Freedom from Religion Freaks when you need them? Or the American Humanist Association? They left us flat. Why don't they come out and threaten to sue the president for reading from the Bible or using God bless America? Because they're cowards. But that's a story for another time.

The president then went on to insinuate that the Voting Rights Act had been trampled on by asking people to simply prove who they are. And this is somehow setting black Americans back 50 years? I'm not going to beat it to death, but even the Supreme

Selma march proves police are racist?

Court in their ruling against the DOJ's authority to step into states' business before any rights are violated said that we do not have the same problems today as we did when it was enacted. (U.S. Supreme Court ruled 5-4 in June 2013 in a case from Shelby County, Alabama, eliminating the Justice Department's ability under the Voting Rights Act to identify and stop potentially discriminatory voting laws before they take effect.)

President Obama himself on a radio interview in October of 2014 said, *"Most of these laws are not preventing the overwhelming majority of folks who don't vote from voting."* Obama said during the interview with Rev. Al Sharpton, *"Most people do have an ID. Most people do have a driver's license. Most people can get to the polls. It may not be as convenient, it may be a little more difficult."* (Insert cricket sound here.) Well, we're done here! You believe the president about everything else why not this?

Most Americans feel you should have a picture ID to vote, as long as the states make them easy to obtain. That doesn't mean you walk up to the window, tell them who you are, and get your ID. Even former President Jimmy Carter and former Secretary of State James Baker agreed, photo ID's are necessary to stop voter fraud.

Yes, President Obama used Selma to talk politics. On a day that important, and with such meaning in U.S. history, can't we just stay away from political agendas? Can't we simply applaud and appreciate all the work that Dr. King and his team accomplished?

Wouldn't this have been the perfect opportunity, for Mr. Obama to jump on that great man's coat tails and push for peaceful protests, stronger family values, less dependence on government, and more reliance on family and church? Those are things that unite both sides, rather than further divide.

RAMBLINGS

I have to wonder if the president has the same fortitude and conviction that Dr. King had. Would he be willing to lay his life down for righteousness and freedom for everyone? To quote from the same book the president did, *"Greater love hath no man than this that a man lay down his life for his friends."*

I don't believe he would, but I've been wrong before!

Chapter 5

PC Police or Political Mafia

In December 2015, we had what some are calling the second worst terror attack on American soil since 9/11. In the end, 14 dead and 21 injured at a holiday office party in San Bernardino, CA. It took a very long time for most of the mainstream, left-leaning media to call it what it was... an attack by extreme, religious, Muslim terrorists. Period!

What were they waiting for? They had no problem calling it an attack by three white guys in ski masks moments after it happened, while they were still being looked for. Then it was workplace violence because one of the shooters supposedly got into a fight with co-workers and came in on the "spur of the moment" on a shooting rampage. And then we heard that it might have been conservative, gun-toting, Christian nutjobs!

ALL of that speculation was A-OK with little to no information. But when Syed Farook was the first suspect name released, not one of the mainstream morons would say, "Maybe we have a terrorist issue, maybe they killed in the name of Islam." Why not?

Why is it OK to assume it's always the white, Christian, conservative Republican? Why? Because we don't behead, kill, stone, or throw gay people off buildings. We don't walk up to you and shoot you in the head because you can't recite a verse from the Bible.

Do we have the occasional nutjob? YES!!!! God yes!!! But we come out in numbers to speak against them. Where are the "numbers" of moderate Muslims speaking out against this?

The PC police have made sure that you feel bad, not only about being white but, if you even have a thought about it being a Muslim-backed or Muslim-based terror attack simply because they're from the Middle East, their name is Mohammed, or they have a Quran, then you're a "hater" and you must be silenced.

As much as the mainstream media were tripping over themselves not to call it a terror attack, even though everything pointed to it, can you IMAGINE what would have happened if, when the police entered the home, they found a Bible and scriptures on the walls? Every station (except maybe FoxNews) would have been talking about the Christian terrorists. No doubt in my mind.

To all you Progressive "Lefties" who love to blame everything on Conservatives, shame on you. You have the blood of 14 innocent murdered people on your hands. You have responsibility for the 21 wounded on your hands.

Two separate individuals, a delivery man and a neighbor, stated that they saw very suspicious activity going on at the suspects' residence and didn't report it. Why? Because YOU, the PC pinheads, have convinced the weak of mind that they are racists or Islamophobes for even considering it. Even when common sense would draw that conclusion.

~ ~

Why? Because YOU, the PC pinheads, have convinced the weak of mind that they are racists or Islamophobes for even considering it.

~ ~

Shame on you for putting that on them. You blame the NRA president for promoting mass murder and have even lumped him in with some of the most notorious killers in America, yet you are willing to give a pass to those who say, "We hate Americans," "We hate what you stand for," "We hate your way of life and we will kill you every chance we get!"

You want to give them jobs, places to live, hugs, and love. Do it over there! Go to their country and help them. Show ISIS the love you speak of. Let me know how that works out for you.

Political correctness is a dangerous and deadly thing. Stop it. And stop it now. San Bernardino is a great community. People are just trying to live out the American dream. Look where political correctness got them!

The PC police have the blood of these and many more on their hands. How many times after these mass shootings have people said, "He was odd and sometimes very angry, but I didn't think it was OK for me to report it." Really? If you're on a college campus, and you have an "odd duck," and they go from zero to out-of-control in a few seconds, and you believe them to be capable of violence... REPORT THEM!

What's really interesting is, there are many on the Left who have reported me to some of the organizations that I serve on as potentially dangerous to some groups because I don't fall in line with their beliefs. They have no problem reporting me. They don't like what I write... they report me. Those same hypocrites come unglued on me for calling out Bruce-Caitlyn Jenner for getting unearned awards or for calling out the Supreme Court on their rulings. Why? Because what I say might, just MIGHT cause someone else to behave violently, even though I repeatedly say violence is never the answer.

However, even after 14 people were murdered and 21 injured on our soil, even after 150+ were executed in Paris and others mowed down and blown up in the name of Allah, we still have to choose our words carefully so as not to offend moderate Muslims. Hypocrites! All of you who think that way are hypocrites. Equality my foot! You don't want equality. You think of yourselves so highly that you believe you get to set the PC standards and the rest of us should fall in line. That's not equality. That's oppression. And I will never just "fall in line."

Now Leftists have another ally in the White House. One that subscribes to using the U.S. Constitution as toilet paper because the only law that matters is what she says is law. Hey Loretta, here's your first case to go after. Our U.S. Attorney General, Loretta Lynch has said the Department of Justice will prosecute any Muslim bashing. In other words, if you say anything bad about Muslims, the AG may step in. Forget local law enforcement. The AG knows better. And she wants you to call them directly! What about Christians? Jews? Blacks? The LGBTQ community? Can they also call the DOJ directly and be afforded the same protections?

Mr. President, your true colors are becoming brighter and brighter. Your love for those of the Muslim faith and the Muslim community far outweigh your love for America and all Americans.

You don't even try to hide it anymore.

Chapter 6

Flush Honor and Integrity?

It seems like the more I do stories about our institutions of higher learning, the more I come to the conclusion that there are no real standards for those teaching our young people. You may need a degree in order to teach, but that's about all. Honor and integrity are no longer required.

Once again, my home state of Massachusetts showed that no matter how bad one's character is, as long as they have a degree and are flaming Liberals, they're in! Boston University first realized they had an issue with incoming BU sociology professor, Saida Grundy, when a Tweet she sent out was brought to the administration's attention: "white male college students are a "problem population"" and "white masculinity is THE problem for America's colleges." She is a black college professor, not that that should matter. As a professor, she is supposed to have open dialogue with her students. Can you imagine if a white college professor Tweeted, "black male college students are a problem population and their entitlement mindset is a MAJOR problem for American colleges?" They'd have been fired before the moving truck got there!

Well, OK. So maybe we're being a little sensitive about the color thing. She got a little heated. We can just overlook her one indiscretion, right? But it wasn't one or two or even three. And let's not stop at four, but six... that we know of! You see, Professor Grundy thinks (like Hillary) that rules, guidelines, and basically good behavior do not apply to her.

The professor decided to mercilessly ridicule a white rape victim on social media with the following;

> *"^^THIS IS THE S**T I AM TALKING ABOUT. WHY DO YOU GET TO PLAY THE VICTIM EVERY TIME PEOPLE OF COLOR AND OUR ALLIES WANT TO POINT OUT RACISM. my*

CLAWS?? Do you see how you just took an issue that WASNT about you, MADE it about you, and NOW want to play the victim when I take the time to explain to you some s**t that is literally $82,000 below my pay grade? And then you promote your "white girl tears" like that's some badge you get to wear... YOU BENEFIT FROM RACISM. WE'RE EXPLAINING THAT TO YOU and you're vilifying my act of intellectual altruism by saying i stuck my "claws" into you?"

HELLO! The woman was raped as a child. And when the rape victim under attack tried to bow out gracefully, the professor tried to pull her back in with more nasty comments. Since the professor makes $82,000 and is above the raped woman's pay grade, shouldn't she have taken the high road? She could have taken her educated backside out of the conversation and just dropped it. Is this really someone we want teaching our young people? Maybe they could have found someone with a little empathy or compassion?

This perfect specimen of a well-educated human being apparently felt that "white" people have so much privilege that she was going to get back at them, or at least one of them. How? Identity theft! At first she would not admit it was her, but the truth eventually caught up with her. In 2007, Grundy, in a fit of jealous rage, decided to sign up a Virginia woman for as many "tryst" sites as possible. She wanted to humiliate the woman. She published the woman's personal information on sites that endangered the woman's life. That's not according to Joe, but according to the police department!

Eventually, Grundy was charged with identity theft and the use of computers to commit a crime (both felonies). Grundy pleaded guilty to a misdemeanor count in exchange for the dismissal of the felonies. Her probation ended in June 2009. Now, 8 years later, we're supposed to forget and move on. That would be fine, if she'd changed. But she started stirring things up again!

Does this mean as long as you're a black female academic you can do no wrong? Does that mean everything is fair game? Even to the point of ridiculing a "white" rape victim? And where's the apology for the victim?

What a great role model for our young minds, right? As if that weren't enough, Professor Grundy also said that she "tries to avoid shopping at white-owned businesses." (You can't make this stuff up!) Only after several alumni complaints, Boston University president Robert Brown condemned the racist Tweets sending an email to faculty, "We are disappointed and concerned by statements that reduce individuals to stereotypes on the basis of a broad category such as sex, race, or ethnicity." Even so, the school refused to rescind her employment offer.

~ ~

Make sure you are a hateful, nasty, vicious, Liberal professor looking for work at a university and you're in! People with honor and integrity need not apply!

~ ~

In a message from BU's African American Studies, faculty welcomed Grundy, saying she had been hired after a nationwide search and chosen from over 100 applicants. The post mentioned Grundy's Tweets and said they've been *"shocked by the number of voicemails left and the hostile emails sent to our office and our individual accounts... However, most troubling was that among the numerous that were serious expressions of dismay were many vile messages, explicitly racist and obscene, that consider cyber-bullying a substitute for frank discussion and freedom of speech."*

RAMBLINGS

Did you catch that? Faculty members were more upset by the tone of the emails and voice messages from those opposed to Grundy's employment than the ugly, hateful things Grundy had actually done and even admitted to doing!

What's a sane person to conclude? Make sure you are a hateful, nasty, vicious, Liberal professor looking for work at a university and you're in!

People with honor and integrity need not apply!

Chapter 7

Global Warming and OZ

I would like to know how many times one has to get predictions wrong before we kick them to the curb? In the Old Testament when a prophet said he had a word from God and it didn't happen, they stoned him! 2015 marked the 15th anniversary of Al Gore's prediction in front of a German audience that the *"North Polar Ice Cap would be completely ice free in five years"* and that *"the entire North 'polarized' cap will disappear in 5 years."*

When that didn't work out, he predicted it again in 2009, *"Some of the models suggest that there is a 75 percent chance that the entire north polar ice cap, during some of the summer months, could be completely ice-free within the next five to seven years."* We're still waiting.

With something as "important" as "Global-Warming-Cooling-Climate-Change" you would think we'd want accuracy and real numbers.

For someone who has been leading this "war," Mr. Al Gore has gotten it wrong every time. Yet those who have made him lord and savior don't care. They keep following him off the cliff like he can save them.

And then, Al Gore got together with the U.N. (United Nuts, they're made for each other!) and raised the alarm. They screamed from the mountain tops that we had less than a decade to save the planet.

The San Jose Mercury News reported on June 30, 1989 that *"senior environmental official at the United Nations, Noel Brown, says entire nations could be wiped off the face of the earth by rising sea levels if global warming is not reversed by the year 2000."*

RAMBLINGS

Well, global warming wasn't even touched, let alone reversed. And the only nations wiped out were those taken by the Russians or ISIS. But hey, don't let facts stop you.

Fifteen years later they were still selling it. They don't even say they made a mistake, it was bad data, a miscalculation... nothing. Just trust us, it's true.

George Monbiot, another "environmentalist," said because we won't fix this issue that within 10 years, farming worldwide would only be able to feed either animals or humans, not both. In 2002 the worldwide numbers of people that went underfed were around 930 million. In 2014 that number dropped to 805 million. I'm not the sharpest knife in the drawer, but I think that's more people eating enough food? What happened? It must be Common Core math! Check out the numbers at the U.N. for yourself.

Another U.N. golden boy, Rajendra Pachauri, the former head of the Intergovernmental Panel on Climate Change said, *"If we don't make changes within the next 3 years it will be too late."* That was 2007. By 2012 we did nothing and the "too Late" (whatever that was) never happened. Now it's 2015 and we're still waiting for a real plan. And Mr. Pachauri (who was the leading Climate Change scientist for the U.N.) was more interested in chasing women around his office than taking care of the "too late" issue. He had to resign due to sexual harassment charges.

Prince Charles weighed in in July of 2009 and warned of *"irretrievable climate and ecosystem collapse, and all that goes with it."* He went on to say that experts had told him we had about 26 months before utter catastrophe. September 2011 came and went. Yep, you guessed it. Nothing happened!

In 2009, UK Prime Minister Gordon Brown said, *"There are only 50 days to take action or global warming would be irreversible."*

He had no Plan B. It's pretty hard to get the entire world to move in 50 days.

Remember the Climate Treaty of 2009? World Leaders came together, again, to save the world. Canadian Prime Minister and Green Party leader said, *"Earth has a long time. Humanity does not. We need to act urgently. We no longer have decades; we have hours."* In all fairness, he didn't actually say how many hours!

When Obama was elected many said he had only 4 years to save the world (what a powerful man.) He had total control of the government those first couple of years and did nothing. U.N. Foundation President Tim Wirth said Obama's second term was *"the last window of opportunity to impose policies to restrict fossil fuel use"* and that it's *"the last chance we have to get anything approaching 2 degrees centigrade, if we don't do it now, we are committing the world to a drastically different place."* That was in 2012.

~ ~

"We only have 500 days to act and avoid a climate chaos."

~ ~

In 2014, France's foreign minister said, *"We only have 500 days to act and avoid a climate chaos."* Swung on and missed! You see, his meeting was in May of 2014. The Climate Change meeting happened December 2015. Over 560 days with no major calamity!

The U.N. and others have been repeating the same mantra at us for years... act now or else. Many times we haven't "acted now" and nothing has happened. No major catastrophes.

RAMBLINGS

They said we would be covered in snow and ice and much of the U.S. would be uninhabitable. That was in the seventies. They called it Global Cooling. They blew it.

Then they told us that it was Global Warming, that New York would be covered with over 50 feet of water, and there would be no ice at the polar ice caps. Another miss!

So they renamed it to Climate Change so they wouldn't have to worry about accuracy. From now on, everything that happens in the weather world is due to Climate Change. Less Hurricanes. Climate Change. More hurricanes. Climate Change. Snow in June. Climate Change. Floods in June. Climate Change. Less  earthquakes. Climate Change. More earthquakes. Climate Change. Get it?

Let me help out. You're making Al Gore and others very rich! Meanwhile, the Earth continues on its natural 5 gabillion year cycle, just as it always has!

Chapter 8

The Left Says We Can't Say... Well, Anything!

When elected, Mr. Obama said...

> *"...from the rocky coast of Maine to the sunshine of California, we are five days away from fundamentally transforming the United States of America..."*

Who knew the gravity of what he was saying? Of what he meant?

Forget for the moment, all of the very in-your-face policies this president has introduced or forced on us that have failed miserably. Let's look at the effect this president and his extreeeeeemely corrupt administration have had on the youth of this nation.

On campuses across the country we have seen unrest like never before. I know, some of you are going to say, "What about the hippies and the 60's, Joe?" And I'll just say, "But the 60's were about protesting war and encouraging more love for one another."

Today, it's about word games and attacks on any norm of the day. Words like marriage, man, woman, girl, boy, and senior citizen are under attack. No, I'm not kidding.

Kids on campus can tell you the definition of "cisgen" but have no clue when the United States gained independence as a country, when we fought that war, and who it was against!

The mentality has become "what's in it for me" instead of "what's good for all." History, optimism, and the American Dream are apparently no longer taught on our college campuses. It has been replaced with classes, seminars, and entire weeks focused on sexual orientations, social microaggressions, white privilege, only black lives matter, and every other manner of political correctness.

Many professors in mainstream colleges are so intent on making white people feel bad about what has been done in the name of "whiteness" and making sure they know about their "white privilege" that they fail to teach the subjects they were hired to teach. One actually said, *"This won't end until all old, white men are*  *dead."* Naw… that won't spark any racist issues on campus, will it?

We can't say things like, "If you work hard, you can be anything you want to be in this country." Why? According to one well-educated professor, because that will offend African Americans. Not Asians, Italians, or Mexicans? Nope. Just African Americans! SERIOUSLY?! Isn't that a racist comment in and of itself? Aren't you saying African Americans aren't smart enough? Or maybe it's just that "the man" will keep them down? How does that apply to Mr. Obama, Mr. Holder, Gen. Collen Powell, Ms. Condoleezza Rice, Ms. Oprah Winfrey, and Mr. Sean Combs? They weren't kept down. And what about these multi-billionaires: Michael Jordan, Mohamed Ibrahim (cell phone company CEO), Michael Lee-Chin (investment firm

The Left Says We Can't Say... Well, Anything!

CEO), Ursula Burns (Xerox CEO, apparently they only care about how much green this black woman can bring in!)

Did you know the first female self-made millionaire was a black woman? And at a time when most were lucky to make a week's pay cleaning houses? Sarah Breedlove, also known as Madam C.J. Walker, experienced hair loss at an early age. In just 12 years, she developed a haircare salve and turned a job as a washer earning $1.50 per day into a hair-care empire. As if that weren't impressive enough, prior to her death in 1919, she put her money to good use actively supporting anti-lynching campaigns and forwarding black education.

Apparently, if you work hard, you can be anything you want to be... including a millionaire! I can post another 100 stories about men and women who are home-grown success stories. But most people prefer to buy the spoon-fed garbage the mainstream media gives them.

They want us to stop using phrases like "melting pot" or "the most qualified person should get the job." These have somehow become derogatory? Melting pot was understood to mean all were welcome and would fit in together (legally) to make a better country. And do you REALLY not want the most qualified person when it comes to hiring airplane pilots, doctors, or lawyers?

Some colleges, like the University of New Hampshire, have now created a list of commonly used words and phrases that are "problematic." They say the term "American" is a problem because it infers that America is the only country on this continent. To the rest of us, it simply means the country we know as the United States. Loons!

They prefer we use "European American" instead of "Caucasian" because all whites are from Europe, right? You know, like all blacks are from Africa... oh wait, maybe not!

"Mothering" and "fathering" are offensive because people must "avoid gendering a non-gendered activity." Should kids now say Parent One and Parent Two?

"Homosexual" is "an outdated clinical term considered derogatory and offensive by many gay and lesbian people." The school administration thinks "Same Gender Loving" should be used instead. (Are they still allowed to say "gay" and "lesbian"? Because they just did!)

"Senior citizen" is bad, but "people of advanced age" is good. Who decided this? Did they take a poll of senior citizens? Did they reach out to the gay and lesbian groups or did they at least call the NAACP and ask if blacks were offended by the terminology? No. Of course they didn't because like their leaders and saviors, these hard-core, Left groups, are the PC police. They see themselves as the keeper of the First Amendment rules and enforcement, so they can just change the rules as they go along.

~ ~

Left groups, are the PC police. They see themselves as the keeper of the First Amendment rules and enforcement, so they can just change the rules as they go along.

~ ~

But don't ask them about basic American History!

The loons are running the asylum. Professors on the far Left and many of those in education that push socialism feel empowered by their socialist leader Mr. Obama to be

35

able to push this line of thinking on trusting, impressionable students.

Some of you on the Left are proud that these young men and women (or whatever they want to be called, I'm sure I just insulted about half of them) are trying to do away with supposedly old, outdated terms. But with all the things our young people are facing after college... lack of jobs, high cost housing, mega debt, mega taxation, and more, why does it seem like all they're learning in college is what to call the greeter at Walmart?

Chapter 9

Did you hate your kids too?

Did you know, preachers in Canada have been arrested for simply teaching Biblical principles as it pertains to homosexuality? There was said nothing about hating the person. No comments about beheading the person. No comments about stoning the person. No reference to acting out in a violent way against anyone in the LGBTQ community. They were simply teaching what God said about homosexuality according to the Bible.

Yet that is considered "hate speech" because it calls the actions of another human being a sin.

Well, first I have to say, if you don't believe in God, then you don't believe in sin. So why are you upset? Next I would ask, how is it hate speech to say the actions of a person are against God?

Is it hate speech if I say I don't like Mexican food? It gives me bad gas and I really just don't like it. Does that mean I hate Mexicans? Because I think the Mexican border should be secured and people should come here legally, does that mean I hate Mexicans? How petty

of you to think that I want the border secured to keep out Mexicans when it's been proven that people from all over the world come over the border illegally.

I posted this statement on social media *"It's already happening in Canada, pastors being arrested for preaching against homosexuality."* Then I asked people to define "hate speech." I got the usual "low IQ" responses; "anything that comes out of your mouth," "anything a Republican says," "anything a conservative says" and so on. One follower named Chris took an honest stab at it... well, as honest as a left-leaning progressive can.

> *"hate speech is anything that incites violence ... also specifically its hate speech when you do things like compare gays to pedophiles and people who have sex with animals.*
>
> *"...if they weren't producing hate speech there would be no problems."*

Well, I have never heard any preacher (except the right Reverend Al Sharpton) advocate violence. Inciting violence in today's society is easy. Make fun of someone's baseball team in the parking lot after a game and you might get your head bashed in and end up in a coma (like what happened at a Los Angeles Dodgers game a few years back). Were the attackers charged with hate crimes? No!

A liberal professor tore up an "anti-abortion" display on campus while calling the young men and woman there all kinds of names. Was she brought up on hate charges? Nope!

~ ~

When a "conservative religious type" says something that offends, they should be brought up on hate speech charges.

~ ~

So, in all honesty, he should have said when a "conservative religious type" says something that offends, they should be brought up on hate speech charges.

RAMBLINGS

Webster's says, pedophilia is "a psychiatric disorder in which an adult or older adolescent experiences a primary or exclusive sexual attraction to prepubescent children, generally age 11 years or younger." Not Joe's definition. So are you saying that no gays or lesbians are pedophiles? And if that is what you're saying, would you say the same about heterosexuals? Or do the same rules not apply?

This is classic, *"...if they weren't producing hate speech there would be no problems."* Where do we live in Whoville? And I suppose we all eat rainbows and poop butterflies?

Wake up! Someone, somewhere will always be offended by something someone somewhere says. Why? Because they choose to be offended and intolerant!

What Left-logic says is that if I don't accept the way you want to live, the things you want to do, and your belief system over mine, then I'm a hater. Period!

If I believe that abortion is wrong and that it's actually taking a human life, I'm a woman hater. If I don't believe in same-sex marriage, I hate same-sex couples.

According to Left-logic, I hate my children. And so did many of you reading this. I have promised the kids I would not give away their deep dark secrets, and I won't. But, when one was dabbling in drugs I told them I wouldn't support them. I even had them arrested for having drugs on them. OMG! Where is child protective services when you need them? According to Left-logic, I hated them.

When one decided they knew how they wanted to live and wouldn't abide by the house rules, they were asked to leave the premises, and they did. According to Left-logic, I hated them.

When one, who usually made great decisions for their life, made a few bad financial decisions after being told what the consequences were going to be for doing exactly what they did, we would not step in to save them. According to Left-logic, I hated them.

Simply put, your "real" definition of hate speech is, "anything someone on the Right says or does that goes against your way of thinking, and irritates you." That's hate speech. How tolerant and fair of you!

I won't be getting on that train.

Chapter 10

The LEFT Wants Facts?

This book wouldn't be complete without a chapter devoted to Hillary Clinton's "misspeaks," "misleads," "what difference, at this point, does it make," and "there were no classified emails on the server." These sagas continue to be in the news, and I do mean the REAL news.

The news gods may be having a little change of heart. ABC, NBC, CBS, and, yes, even MSNBC have been asking questions and making comments about Hillary's blatant disregard for the law and her failure to think things through when it comes to taking money from countries and questionable characters.

Just when I thought the clouds were going to part and some sanity set in, in steps George Stephanopoulos, a very left-wing journalist, who, after speaking with the author of "Clinton Cash" basically said, "Move along nothing to see here." His whole premise is that since we have no hard evidence that money changed hands for favors through the White House for the Clintons that all is well in Oz.

~ ~

It used to be that journalists gave us all sides of the issue and allowed us to draw a conclusion. They didn't decide what the truth was and then paint a picture that would lead us to their truth.

~ ~

Well, Mr. Stephanopoulos, all is not well in Oz. And you, sir, are a MAJOR part of the problem. It used to be that journalists gave us all sides of the issue and allowed us to draw a conclusion. They didn't decide what the truth was and then paint a picture that would lead us to their truth.

The LEFT Wants Facts?

This same group of mainstream media people made many assumptions about George W Bush and had no problem accusing him while "misspeaking" their facts as truth.

Mr. Stephanopoulos is floored that anyone would draw any conclusion of wrongdoing starting with Mrs. Clinton's email issue. She simply made a mistake and since the president knew about it, all is well! Really? Turn the tables and see what would have happened if it had been done by a Republican.

Nothing "fishy" about Mr. Clinton getting, on average, $70,000 for speaking gigs before Hillary became Secretary of State. But

after her appointment, all of a sudden he is worth $500,000 to $1.3 million per speaking gig. Did he take a speech writing class? Get better Teleprompters? That's not

important. And no worries, most of those were events with some connection to donors.

In the immortal words of Yul Brynner in the "King and I"... "eeez a puzzlement."

Here's a quick rundown...

- Kingdom of Saudi Arabia, $25 million to the Clinton Foundation for the betterment of the Clintons.
- Australia, $10 million to the Clinton Foundation for the betterment of the Clintons.
- Sultanate of Oman, $5 million to the Clinton Foundation for the betterment of the Clintons.

- And the list goes on to the tune of $150 million to the Clinton Foundation for the betterment of the Clintons (CFFTBOTC).

Who else? What other legislator? What other past president? What other past legislator has received this kind of money from foreign entities? I'll save you the time... NO ONE! Donations are made to Presidential Libraries for the purpose of upkeep and purchasing artifacts for the library, not the presidential families. But Georgie says you have nothing that actually ties to an agreement to provide services.

A uranium (shell) company donated big bucks to the CFFTBOTC. Shortly after the donation, coincidentally, Mrs. Clinton changed her mind about the U.S. blocking the uranium mining deal and even encouraged such deals in some of her speeches.

Then, there is the "refiling" of past tax returns. Since it was brought to their attention that they forgot to include many, if not all, of the Canadian deal-based donations on their reports. Let's pause here a minute. Hillary says she is a person of integrity and ethics. They have an elite team managing this foundation. How did they miss MILLIONS of dollars in donations with such an experienced team of employees at The Foundation? Not once, not twice, but 4 years in a row! Tax experts say it's highly unusual for a foundation to refile this many years because of omissions.

Well, not to worry. Hillary stepped down from the foundation's board of directors within a few months of the allegations but her husband, Bill, and their daughter, Chelsea, remain directors. I'm sure she will keep and arm's length (or at least a bedroom length) away from Bill and the foundation. After all, she has always been honest and up front with us on all issues, right?

That whole, Benghazi debacle where she swears they never refused to send help. Oh wait... never mind! OK, then there is the "I turned over all the correspondence and emails pertaining to

The LEFT Wants Facts?

Benghazi and my term as Secretary of State" thing. Oh, wait... never mind. At least she only erased the emails that had to do with her daughter's wedding, her aunt's death, her yoga routines, and her personal transactions on the homes they purchased. Yep, all 33,000 of those personal emails. Oh, wait... never mind. OK then, we'll just track down the entities and people she *probably* sent emails to and ask them for them... guess what? The first dozen or so refused to share. Bet you can't see my shocked face?

They'd have you believe that there is nothing to see here. Just step away from the curtain!

You on the Left pitched a fit and wanted to see former Republican presidential candidate Mitt Romney's tax return because Senator Harry Reid lied about someone telling him Romney didn't pay taxes. You hypocrites have no outrage over Hillary's deceptive disclosure because, as Harry put it, you won!

This stench will continue to grow. Hillary can't keep lying to cover up all of these messes. And you honest Democrats out there (yes, there are honest ones) if you cover up for her (them) you are just as guilty of all the death and destruction they've left in their wake.

The REAL facts show that they are guilty of not caring for America, not caring for women, not caring for the poor or sick, but just caring for the Clintons. How can you keep voting for them?

Chapter 11

Christian Extremists? SERIOUSLY?

It seems like most articles written of late mention how Christians are ignoring their terrible recent past where MANY Christians have killed in the name of their religion. I would call that a falsehood, but simply put... it's a lie.

Years ago, my wife and I took a parenting class. We had a "blended" home and wanted to learn how to parent effectively. In that class, we learned about "deflection," used expertly by teens far and wide. It goes something like this: as you are correcting Little Johnny, he brings up the fact that Little Susie did something that you let her get away with. He is trying to deflect the heat off himself. In the class we learned the response should always be, "nevertheless, we are dealing with you" and don't defend the intended deflection argument.

Many people claim to be Christian or to follow Christianity, yet they've never killed, maimed, raped, or otherwise injured others in the name of Christ or God. Never have I seen training videos of Christian camps teaching their children how to hate and kill others. Never have I seen Christians beheading others who don't believe. Never have I seen Christians performing female genital mutilation in the name of God or yelling "Praise Jesus" while they are mowing down people in a mall or concert hall.

~ ~ ~ ~ ~ ~ ~ ~ ~ ~ ~ ~ ~ ~ ~ ~ ~ ~ ~ ~

Never have I seen training videos of Christian camps teaching their children how to hate and kill others.

~ ~ ~ ~ ~ ~ ~ ~ ~ ~ ~ ~ ~ ~ ~ ~ ~ ~ ~ ~

Yes, I have seen, heard, and read about some extreme Christian crazies (notice how I am not afraid of using the word "extreme" when needed) who blew up an abortion clinic because God hates abortion. Well, God does hate abortion, but He also hates blowing up clinics with innocent people in it. There are NO scriptures in the New Testament that call for this or any other kind of violence. The Bible actually states that "vengeance is mine says the Lord." A true follower of Christ would leave it up to God because He can do a much better job.

Those who argue that Christians have murdered more people than anyone will immediately throw out Timothy McVeigh's name. You have to go back decades to find even that one. He grew up Catholic, as many of us did, and in an interview he stated, *"I grew up Catholic as a young child, but never really practiced the religion."* He told the authors of "American Terrorist" that he "did not believe in Hell." If there's one tenet that's consistent with Christian religions, it's a belief in Hell—and Heaven, for that matter.

And then there are those who insist that Hitler was a Christian. Talk about reaching! He, too, grew up Catholic. But Hitler believed in Nazism. He believed, according to his book, that though there was evidence of a creator, ultimately, man and god became one. That's not a Christian belief... at all! He thought he was doing the work of the creator by exterminating the Jews. How can that possibly be a Christian viewpoint when the Bible clearly states that Jews are God's chosen people? It can't.

I also love those who study nothing in the Bible but throw out-of-context Bible verses at a situation that has nothing to do with the verse. I recently saw one that showed Christians helping little kids. The person alluded to the fact that people following Christ are ignoring Him if we don't allow refugee children and women into our country. Where is that in the Bible, exactly? Is it the verse where Christ basically said that *"it would be better for a millstone to be put around your neck and be thrown into the sea than you hurt a little child?"*

RAMBLINGS

Let's start off with the verse where Jesus talks about "rendering unto Caesar." In other words, you obey the laws of the land! We have immigration laws! Then let's talk about what Jesus really said because He has lots to say about social issues, like if a man won't work he won't eat! Like a working man is worthy of his wages (my Bible is not gender neutral, sorry). Give a man a fish he eats for a night, teach him to fish he can feed himself, his family, and maybe even his neighbors. (I added a few.) Nothing really about handouts. Actually, many time He uses the word "you". YOU go and preach. YOU go and teach. YOU go and sin no more. Get the gist?

The acts of these individual, so-called Christian, idiot extremists don't even espouse the mainstream belief of the religion they claim to follow. And in all cases, none of them yelled "God is great" in any language. If you add up 25 years of so-called killing in the name of Christ worldwide you can't come near the number of those killed in the name of Allah in the last 3 years alone!

No one I know says ALL Muslims are bad or killers. No one! However, ALL Muslim extremists are bad and killers. They always kill in the name of Allah. They will NOT live peaceably with all men. TODAY they still stone women for being raped, throw gays off the roofs of buildings, light people on fire alive, and behead. Shall I go on? And all in the name of Allah.

Now some of you are going to say, Joe, they aren't following the real teachings of their book just like you say Christian extremists don't follow yours. You are correct! However, when a Christian does something stupid and horrible in the name of God or openly says it's because of his or her religion, I and MANY others speak out against them. We have no problem because, though we believe in forgiveness, we also believe you pay for your crimes. However, where is the concentrated outrage of the REAL Muslims when real hate is shown in the name of Allah?

There have been 3600 people killed, in America, in the name of Allah and another 1700 who survived killing attempts by Muslim extremists on American soil from 1972 until July 2015.

I'm sorry, there's no comparison. We need to be vigilant. And EVERY ONE, every refugee gets checked out before coming into our country!

Chapter 12

Progressive American Propaganda...

on a College Campus near You

Each week I am inundated with emails from people all over the country with stories that are "out of this world." Some are so deep in conspiracy theories that, if compiled, we would have a fantastic science fiction novel. But let's deal with a little reality, truth, and fact!

Look at what's happening on our college campuses. Jewish students being arrested at a peaceful protest for inciting a riot. They did nothing. Violence was started by the opposition because they wanted the Jewish students to stop "spreading their propaganda." Wow, really!? On our college campuses? Where free thought and the free flow of ideas are openly welcomed? REALLY? Or recently, at a California college, a Jewish student was denied acceptance to a committee. Not because she was unqualified, but because she was Jewish. Yep. So much for institutes of higher learning and reason.

Where are the professors and administrators while all this is going on? Sitting around their little Lib think-tanks, or should I say, "Devoid of Rational Thought Tanks." There is little to no pushback from Liberal academia. Why? From what I have read, it's because they are smarter than us! It's because we are too uneducated to work it through without the help of anyone from "their world." Any professors who take a more conservative stance on issues are immediately ridiculed and pushed out. Once again I say, so much for freedom of thought and free flowing ideas on campus.

It seems most of these campuses have become little Liberal concentration camps to reprogram those who have lost their way and gone down the Conservative thinking path. They have to be reprogrammed and brought back to a more Liberal way of thinking. Those already in the Liberal Camp are reinforced that all is good in their world.

~ ~

They have to be reprogrammed and brought back to a more Liberal way of thinking.

~ ~ ~ ~ ~ ~ ~ ~ ~ ~ ~ ~ ~ ~ ~ ~ ~ ~ ~ ~

No, you say?

On another wonderful, American campus here in Communist Progressive America, the college is requiring all groups to take LGBTQ training. When one group requested an opt-out they were labeled a hate group! How tolerant of the Left, once again showing their true colors. If I don't agree with you (Liberals), I'm part of a hate group. If you (Liberals) don't agree with me, you're enlightened and I'm just backward. Wow! How unenlightened on your part! I wonder what would happen if they pushed a mandatory "Intro to Religion" class? Whaddaya think, eh? Who's the real bully here?

And if you're not frosted yet, let's look at banning the flag!

Yes, on our college campuses across the country we have an ever-growing group of young men and women who don't really understand how they got there. On one campus in particular, in sunny California, one of the student body groups decided to ban ALL flags from being displayed in prominent places on campus, especially the American Flag because it was a symbol of oppression! The American Flag a symbol of oppression! They have no clue as to what oppression really is. Hey ladies in that group, go over to Iran, Syria, and Saudi Arabia to get a taste of what real oppression looks like. You aren't allowed to appear in public unaccompanied by a male relative or guardian, marry who you want, wear the latest fashion, drive, and in some countries go to school. Go ahead and protest the government there for equal rights. Let me know how that works out for you!

You have the right to be an idiot because of what that American Flag really represents. Many people in years gone by came to this country (and still do) because of the freedom and opportunities it still

represents. Those kids, yes, I say kids because they are acting like children, don't understand that they are on American soil, protected by American police and soldiers, who act on securing their freedom because of the American Constitution, all paid for with American tax dollars. The school gets Federal (American) grants to the tune of almost $30 million a year. In this case, the ban on the Flag was quickly overturned. But still, professors at the school are urging students not to give up the fight to ban our Flag. Another bunch of dishonest Loons.

Look, if you don't like American symbols, you don't see America as the greatest nation on the planet, or you think America is the great oppressor... get your meds checked and then move! No... wait... just move!!!!

Chapter 13

No War on Religion?

Let me start by saying, I understand that there is a physical war in the Middle East on Jews, Christians, and to a degree even Muslims. But what I am dealing with here is the on-going war in this country on Christians.

You separation-of-church-and-state people seem to be very silent on favors provided to other religions, yet start foaming at the mouth when the words "cross," "Bible," "Christ," or any scriptures are used.

A victory for America came when, in 2015, the Freedom from Religion Freaks (aka Freedom from Religion Foundation - FFRF) lost a lawsuit they filed against the 9/11 Memorial Museum. They claimed that displaying the cross found at the bottom of the rubble (not manmade) that served as a symbol of hope to the first responders, Jews, Christians, atheists, and others during that tragedy was a clear violation of the separation of church and state. Once again, they were wrong.

The courts sided with the American people and said that not only was it a symbol of hope, but it was part of our national heritage and history. They said:

> *"[Given] the absence of any evidence of ulterior religious motives, and the undisputed historical significance of The Cross at Ground Zero, we conclude that, as a matter of law, the record compels the conclusion that the actual purpose of displaying the cross in the September 11 Museum is a genuine secular interest in recounting the history of extraordinary events."*

One of the arguments from the atheist group was that the cross caused "dyspepsia" to some of the plaintiffs who had to walk by it. My thought... take some Pepto-Bismol. The ailment equates to an upset stomach.

Then there was the attempt to remove Bibles from U.S. Navy lodges around the globe. The group claimed that offering Bibles to guests constituted an endorsement of a religion so they needed to be removed. I've never heard of anyone walking up and down the lodge halls screaming, "Get your Bibles here, brand new never opened, get 'em while they are free." Nope, not one complaint about Bibles being pushed on anyone. They're in a drawer in each room given free of charge by the Gideon's.

~ ~

"Get your Bibles here, brand new never opened, get 'em while they are free."

~ ~

The people complaining are not being honest. If it was an issue of religious freedom, then let's put the Bible, Quran, Torah, dictionary, or whatever religious text we can get our hands on in those drawers and let them chose what to read or not read. Nope. They only complained that the Bible needed to go. Navy brass came to their senses and backed down because of the outcry of the many as opposed to doing what a very few loud mouths wanted.

In a small town in Georgia, the atheist group threatened to file suit against a school because the kids were praying before football games. They said they had received "a" complaint from a single, unnamed parent. The atheist group was not from the community. They didn't know who they were playing with. Remember, we are supposed to have a representative government, not a government of the smallest and loudest. Well, these people got a taste of southern law. Over 200 people showed up to support the teams in prayer. And they prayed before the game. No one exploded. No one went into convulsions. And no lighting struck any one of them. All was well in that little Georgia town.

The atheists are all legalled-up and ready for battle. Why? Why does something that supposedly doesn't exist make them so crazy? Why can't they respect the wishes of the masses instead of the wishes of a few?

To show how disingenuous they really are (which is an educated way of saying full of manure), the Pentagon recently came down with a ruling that will allow religious garb to be worn on military bases. Not in the field of active duty, but at all other times. We aren't talking about a cross around the neck or a bracelet with a scripture on it or a piece of jewelry or even scarves with the same type of religious markings. Those will still be unacceptable.

Jews have been able to seek a waiver to wear a yarmulke, and since it fits under a helmet or military issued headgear it's not deemed "offensive." The FFRF have many articles about how this is acceptance of religion. But where are they on the new rule allowing Sikhs wearing turbans? They were all over Christians

who outwardly wore crosses or scripture references on their clothing on base. But this? Nothing! There is already a policy where rooms have been designated as prayer rooms. Not

chapels, you know that generic place where all, but Muslims, are expected to use. These are specific rooms set aside for Muslim prayer. But that's OK, right?

RAMBLINGS

The military ordered all chapels to remove all "religious symbols" or hide them so no one could see them. Huh? Isn't that like taking down the "golden arches" at McDonalds? What sense does that make? A chapel without religious symbols? Where is the outcry on the prayer rooms and turbans? Where are the Freedom from Religion Freaks on this one? What if a Christian complained seeing the turban gave them "dyspepsia"? Hmmm, I wonder.

And last but not least, a recent ruling by the brass ordered that all military respect the "religious" tradition of Ramadan by not eating in front of or near any soldier who might be a Muslim. What if my religion requires me to eat more during Ramadan? Where is the outcry from the Freedom from Religion Freaks on this one? Nothing. Why? Because they're cowards. Period. During lent Catholics also fast. Has anyone seen a memo from military brass asking for other members of the military to be sensitive to them? Nope!

It seems to me that if the outcry from all these atheist groups were against religion as a whole then all forms of religious expression would be fought, not just Christian practices.

So, is it a war on religion? No. A war on Christianity, yes!

Chapter 14

They Can Only Win By Lying

It seems like the party of "the people" can only win by lying to "the people."

In an interview back in 2015 Senator Harry Reid admitted that he lied to help Mr. Obama win. He, at this point, is the most honorable man in the Democrat party.

You see, he is the ONLY Democrat to really come out after being caught and basically say… yep, I did it and I got what I wanted, so sue me. He knew the information on Obama's opponent, Mitt Romney was false. There was no "insider" at Romney's company. But he and the rest of the Dems were OK lying about it.

The Democrats should change the name of the party to the "Whatever it takes to win" party. Tell the people whatever it takes to get them "in bed" with you and then you can say "I didn't mean it that way" later.

Obama's now ever-famous and haunting promises about Obamacare, "if you like your doctor, you can keep your doctor" was clearly a LIE! "If you like your plan, you can keep your plan," also a LIE. Then he tried to "clarify" with "What I meant was, if it fit our parameters," yet another LIE!

I think when the NEW edition of "The Book of Lies" gets published the first group of pages will be all Democrats, and mostly Mr. Oblamo! It will be followed closely behind by Billy "where's the free sex island" Clinton's whoppers; "I did not have sexual relations with that woman" and "it depends on what the meaning of is, is." Not far behind is the oh-so-loving spouse, Hillary with "what difference, at this point, does it make" and "there were no classified emails on that server."

If a Republican did one-tenth of what the Clintons have done to the public there would be rioting in the streets, courtesy of the Reverends Al Sharpton and Jesse Jackson.

Recently, Representative Luis Gutierrez from Illinois said, "If the Republicans got in the way of the amnesty order there would be militant action from the immigrants." WHAT?!

Hey, Mr. Gutierrez, did you just threaten American representatives and citizens with militant action from NON-American citizens? Did you just sanction an act of violence to perpetuate the breaking of laws? Aren't you a lawmaker, sworn to uphold the U.S. Constitution? Isn't this a form of treason?

A bunch of Democrats screamed "discrimination" after Indiana enacted a new law protecting peoples' religious beliefs and the practice thereof. Interestingly enough, it's the same reason the original settlers came here... to get away from religious persecution. This group of Dems said no one should patronize, support, or take part in any event or action to support Indiana. Curious!

Some of these same Dems made a trip to Cuba to support the illegal actions of President Obama. In case you haven't figured it out, Mr. Obama and clan believe the Constitution and the laws of this country don't apply to them. They let the Castro Crew know they are in support of Cuba normalizing

relations with America. Well, if the Dems held true to their belief system then that would only occur AFTER the Castro regime changed its laws and treatment of homosexuals, right? And after they changed their laws on the treatment of political prisoners too? Do you think that happened? I think not.

Let's not forget Iran. The president wanted us to believe that the deal (non-deal) he made with Iran was good for everyone involved. It was so good that even the French walked away stating what a bad deal it was. Israeli Prime Minister, Benjamin Netanyahu says it the beginning of the end. The Russians and Chinese left because there was no movement. But our ever-loving, "alternate universe reality," President Obama said we were staying at the table because we were making progress. Usually when one person in the room sees a situation one way and the rest see it another, the odd man out is usually under the influence of narcotics or some other delusion!

The president televised his usual rah-rah speech about how happy and proud he was of his team and this non-deal. Sure, the Iranians got sanctions lifted and all they really had to agree to do is come back to the table with a real plan by a specific deadline. They also agreed to have open weapons inspections, you know, the kind they've agreed to many times in the past and ignored many times in the past with little (or no) consequences. But, President Obama says, it's a good deal for ALL *if* Iran does what they say.

If I made the bets I wanted to make I would be a very wealthy man.

The Iranians have done exactly what we said they would do. They got their money, all bets were off, they are buying warplanes from Russia and missile plans and parts from North Korea. They have tested rockets that were strictly forbidden in the agreement and when outcry came, the Iranian government said: "we were only joking" sorry "my bad" (that's my interpretation!) They said there was no agreement and that they never signed an agreement. And then they said were not going to abide by an agreement that could be changed by a future government. HELLO! I told you so!

I often wonder why Mr. Obama chooses the most communist, hate-filled, anti-human rights countries to build alliances with, all the while shunning and getting in the way of progress with our allies all across the world. Any thoughts? Keep it clean!

We have been blatantly lied to and threatened by, President Obama, Mr. and Mrs. Clinton, Attorney General Eric Holder, Al Gore, and Representative Gutierrez just to name a few. In the time of our Founding Fathers, every one of these individuals would have been brought up on treason charges and disposed of accordingly.

My real issue is that the America-loving Democrats don't come out against their own. It takes an act of God to get them to move. And don't use New Jersey Senator Robert Menendez as the ONE example. He was just a casualty after daring to question the president. Are there no others? Or are they just too afraid after seeing what happened to Menendez? Obama's DOJ chose not prosecute Lois Learner for her part in the IRS scandal. They knew they are required to under the law but chose to ignore it. Menendez, an enemy of their party? YES. And Lois Learner, an enemy of the people but a good "party" soldier got a pass!

Republicans go after themselves to a fault. The Dems never spend money on opposition research because they know they can get all of that from Republicans during the primaries. Most of the time we take our own people to the woodshed and perform public floggings. Just look at what happened during the last presidential primary.

Obama, Holder, Clintons, and many others at the top have lied and cheated on the American people. Is it because they know their message is old and can't win? Is it really the only way they

CAN win? Have they solidified themselves as the party of the untruth?

~ ~

The Dems appear to be "over it" with our laws, our rules, and our protocols. And we really do absolutely nothing to stop them.

~ ~

By their actions, the Dems appear to be "over it" with our laws, our rules, and our protocols. And we really do absolutely nothing to stop them. Democrat leadership is 100% sure they are smarter than us and know what's better for us, so they just repeatedly sidestep the laws. Be honest with yourselves people, even those of you on the Left!

They care more for non-American, lawbreakers than they do for the people who were born here, have paid taxes (their salaries!), and voted them in!

Sadly, it seems the Dems are willing to do anything they can to prove they are right, even if it brings this country to its knees. The question is, are you going to sit idly by and just let it happen, or are YOU going to do something about it?

Note: While writing this book, Iran has broken the "non-signed" agreement several times by firing rockets and purchasing military equipment from other countries. AMAZING!

Chapter 15

Who's Killing Who in the U.S.?
The REAL facts!

Remember when your parents told you to believe half of what you see and almost none of what you hear?

I think of that every time I see a Tweet or Facebook post from people I know never check out their information. These erroneous posts get traction mostly because they are received by friends and family who think you would never send them something that wasn't true. Many have been bitten, including me, because we don't take the time to check it out. Yet it seems when it comes to political issues especially, we never, ever, ever want to challenge loved ones. Well, it's time to start!

One Tweet floated by asking the question, *"What is it with white men in society? Why are so many killing American Muslims, women, blacks, and children?"* This came from a person who has worked in the media and claims that they only speak the truth, but people like me on the Right are wacked!

~ ~ ~ ~ ~ ~ ~ ~ ~ ~ ~ ~ ~ ~ ~ ~ ~ ~ ~ ~

"What is it with white men in society? Why are so many killing American Muslims, women, blacks, and children?"

~ ~ ~ ~ ~ ~ ~ ~ ~ ~ ~ ~ ~ ~ ~ ~ ~ ~ ~ ~

Low IQ voters and those with a victim mentality eat posts like this up. But it's all wrong. I didn't go to any Right-wing sites or Left-wing sites. I went to those highly partisan sites known as the FBI (for crime stats) and the DOJ (for crime reports).

Let's look at a few:

2012 DOJ – The percentages of black adults and white adults arrested for murder were similar, with 49.3 percent being black and 48.3 percent being white.

2012 Black juveniles accounted for 51.5 percent of all juveniles arrested for violent crimes. White juveniles accounted for 61.6 percent of all juveniles arrested for property crimes.

Doesn't look like a wide margin to me!

As I looked for the numbers I found a little-known fact. The DOJ combines Hispanic and white in many statistics. Why? They really can't get percentages on Hispanics because they can't get an actual count on them.

According to a 2009 report by the Pew Hispanic Center, in 2007 Latinos "accounted for 40% of all sentenced federal offenders." This was an increase from 24% in 1991. 72% of the Latino offenders were not U.S. citizens. For Hispanic offenders sentenced in federal courts, 48% were immigration offenses and 37% drug offenses.

According to the US Department of Justice, blacks accounted for 52.5% of homicide offenders from 1980 to 2008, with whites at 45.3% and "other" at 2.2%. The offending rate for blacks was almost 8 times higher than whites (per 100,000), and the victim rate 6 times higher (per 100,000). Most murders were not interracial, with 84% of white homicide victims murdered by whites, and 93% of black victims murdered by blacks. I couldn't find anything saying that most crimes committed by whites were against the various groups of people stated in the false Tweet.

According to the Human Rights Commission, World Health Organization, and Human Rights Watch over 5000 honor killings are committed every year and many of them by the fathers, brothers, and uncles of Muslim women. That means Muslim men are killing Muslim women. Here it is America. You can't find any stats on white men killing Muslims, oh, except maybe the 3 that were killed by a nut a while back. There were 93 honor killings in America, by family members over the past few years. None of them were those pasty, white guys looking to kill Muslim women!

On black crime, the FBI stats don't play out to the Left's lies. FBI statistics indicate that blacks are more likely to commit hate crimes than any other race. According to downtrend.com:

> We are told that because blacks are incarcerated at a disproportionate rate compared to their population that the criminal justice system is racist. We are told that because blacks are suspended from school at a disproportionate rate compared to their population that the education system is racist. Well, what are we to make of this: blacks commit hate crimes at a disproportionate rate to their population.
>
> The FBI recently released the latest <u>hate crime statistics</u> and it doesn't look good for the black community, which is portrayed as America's biggest victim. In 2013, 24.3% of all hate crime offenders were black. According to the last <u>census</u>, blacks make up 12.6% of the population. That means that blacks commit hate crimes at nearly double the rate of their population percentage.
>
> Now let's compare that to whites. The FBI reports that 52.4% of hate crime offenders were white. Keep in mind that the FBI considers Hispanics as whites so the percentage of actual white hate crime offenders is likely much lower. In any case, non-Hispanic whites make up 63.7% of the US population. Throw in the Hispanics and it's 72.4%. Either way, whites commit hates crimes at a rate lower than their population percentage.

The point of all this is not to attack any particular group. It is to simply point out that I'm tired of lazy, hateful people who simply Tweet and post "supposed" facts labeled as truth and then hide in cyberspace. Do your own homework. Let's act on true information, then we can fix the problems in society today.

Chapter 16

Does Right and Wrong exist?

The president frequently resorts to beating on Christians with ridiculously out of context scripture references. Well, Mr. Obama, I have one for you.

> *"Woe to those who call evil good and good evil, who put darkness for light and light for darkness, who put bitter for sweet and sweet for bitter!"* ~ Isaiah 5:20 English Standard Version (ESV)

Basically, woe to the confused who think right is wrong and wrong is right! Mr. Obama, I listened to your carefully chosen words with 2 major international boondoggles... Iran and Cuba.

First, there's Iran. You stated in an interview that you thought it was crazy that the legislators had been out there "spinning" the Iran agreement before it happened (but then you said it did happen over a week before the interview.) You were concerned that legislators thought Iran would not live up to the proposed agreement. Not that that matters. Iran wouldn't put it in writing and the legislators wouldn't sign it anyway!

You also said that the way we've been handling Iran wasn't working and hadn't worked for 30 years. Shouldn't we use an entity's previous track record or "MO" (modus operandi) to anticipate how they would respond? Our military experts do it. Financial experts do it and you've even cited them many times. Business experts do it to predict the market and consumer buying trends. But Obamavision seems to be blind to this. It seems you believe that you have the Midas Touch and everything you do is golden. Actually, I think you're more like Schleprock from the Flintstones. You have a dark cloud that follows you around and everything you get involved with fails!

Does Right and Wrong exist?

You wanted to give Iran a chance because you were sure this time they would actually stick to the agreement. Interestingly, almost every Middle Eastern leader thought you were wrong! Turns out, they were correct and you were wrong. Your crystal ball must have lied to you.

If you had really followed facts you would have considered that in the past they have cheated and lied to U.N. inspectors. But that didn't concern you. The fact that they built an enrichment

facility deep inside a mountain so we couldn't see it didn't concern you either. And neither did the fact that they have been playing war with their navy ships, bombing replicas of American ships. And what about the fact that their leader says there is no agreement, says you are lying, and says that they will not do anything until ALL restrictions are removed? Remember, you said restrictions would be removed gradually. Why didn't you call him out? Prove you didn't lie to us and that you have a spine. Never mind. I knew you wouldn't.

The agreement says we won't be able to inspect their military installations. Does that mean they promised us with a "cross my heart" and a kiss up to Allah that they will not be having any uranium on the bases? To coin an old seventies term, "Sure, I'll still love you in the morning."

Then, there is Cuba. Mr. President, you say we have been handling them the same way for 50 years and it has changed nothing. You're right, I agree! They still oppress their people. The

RAMBLINGS

Castro brothers are still vicious dictators. They still imprison and torture political prisoners. Their 1% percenters are the Castro brothers. They still imprison homosexuals (so much for human rights.) But none of those things bother you. And you think that if we just lighten up and start doing business with them again all that will change?

Don't you think if they really wanted freedom for their people they would have installed, or allowed an election for, a democratic government? Just sayin'!

What do you think normalizing relations with an oppressive, communist, human rights offending government will do for them, and for that matter, us?

Raul Castro wants money and an apology for how we have treated them over the years and I have a sneaky suspicion, Mr. President, that you're trying to figure out how to do that! I'll tell you what, you get them to apologize for the human rights violations they have committed against their people since they took over and you can tell them, well, nothing. We did nothing wrong.

On your visit there you looked like a little boy who finally got to meet his favorite baseball player, his hero. Your speech sounded like you didn't want to upset the Castro Bros. but wanted so show you had some spine. Well, that was a fail. You did, and continue to do, nothing to show those murderous dictators that you will protect democracy or Americans. At least you have been consistent about that.

You tap the phones of our friendly allies and then give a pass to the nations who hate us. You won't help arm or rearm those who are willing to really fight for freedom for their people, but you will allow Iran, another human-rights oppressing, woman and homosexual-hating country to get closer to creating a nuclear weapon.

Mr. Obama, I really am seeing the hate and disdain you have for the American way of life and living.

America has always had issues but has always worked at correcting those issues and mistakes (although maybe not fast enough). We have righted many wrongs. We have even helped our enemies rebuild. We have fed and defended peoples all over the world. We are not the big, bad country that you make us out to be. And still, you continue to beat on us, yes all of us, except a chosen few that you deem worthy.

~ ~

You tap the phones of our friendly allies and then give a pass to the nations who hate us.

~ ~

Newsflash, Mr. President, we will come back. You have awakened a sleeping giant. Even from within your own Party they are seeing the damage you do. And although they can't stand Republicans, they can't stand what you're doing to this country even more!

Next to you, Joe Biden looks like an Oxford Professor, and I am sure former President Jimmy Carter is dancing in his living room knowing when he leaves this earth he will no longer be known as the worst president ever. Your real danger comes from thinking you know more than lifelong military experts, lifelong economic experts, lifelong foreign affairs experts, and that you simply know more than anyone else on the planet!

You have confused right with wrong. You have confused truth and lies. And you are confused as to who the ultimate judgment comes from. As a professing Christian, I am sure you won't mind if I ask my brothers and sisters in Christ to pray for God to open

RAMBLINGS

up your eyes with understanding so you can see what you need to do to make things right again.

Otherwise, move aside and let Joe drive...

Chapter 17

A Lone Gunman Strikes?

In July 2015 we lost 5 of our finest, young men who served our country. Three came back from tours overseas and continued their service encouraging others to do the same.

I have spoken to many of these young men and women asking them why they serve. Why put your life on the line for a cause they often don't seem to get much support for?

The answer is always the same, but it's never the pay! Nope. Not the benefits. Not the education. Or the housing or the food! It has nothing to do with seeing the world or those great uniforms they get to wear. What would possess these young people to serve? Their answer is always; *"We love this country, sir."* They usually go on to say that they want to protect the freedoms this country offers all its citizens and that they still believe this is the best country on the planet.

The never complain about a living wage, living arrangements, work hours, time off, internet access, or sleeping accommodations because they love what they do and they believe that they are doing the right thing.

Do you know where the largest concentration of military recruits come from? The South! Florida, Georgia, South Carolina, North Carolina, Tennessee, Texas, and so on. In the South, approximately 7 out of every thousand people enlist, as opposed to <u>less than</u> 3 out of every thousand from California, New York, and Massachusetts. We've been pummeling Southerners for being racists, yet their actions prove that they love this country (and ALL the people in it) enough to make what could be the ultimate sacrifice. Meanwhile, some of those other states can only complain about the country and those Southern "racists."

Some of our service personnel are seriously injured yet can't wait to get back to the battlefield! And then there are those who simply can't go back to the battlefield.

And how do we honor these people who give their lives for us? By not protecting them! We honor them by ignoring the real and present danger. In other words... we don't honor them at all!

~ ~

How do we honor these people who give their lives for us? By not protecting them!

~ ~

We don't honor them until it's too late. We give them medals for coming home with missing limbs. We honor them by giving a flag to their families when they pay the ultimate sacrifice. We honor them by considering lowering standards so certain groups of people can qualify for elite service units because it's politically correct (something our military should never be). We honor them by turning what was the most respected military force on the planet into a military you might be able to count on if the higher ups give the order in time to make a difference. That's not honor!

President Obama further dishonored our military by not acknowledging what really happened at a recruiting station in Chattanooga, Tennessee in July 2015. Five military men were gunned down by an ISIS sympathizer... on American soil. And our President called it an isolated incident by a "lone gunman."

I've gone from giving him the benefit of the doubt, to calling it what it is... This President is delusional.

He must have meant it was an isolated incident like those Boston bombing cowards who detonated 2 bombs during the Boston

A Lone Gunman Strikes?

Marathon in 2013. You know. Those 2 young men with Muslim extremist connections? Sure. It was that kind of isolated incident.

How about a few other isolated incidents?

September 2014, Oklahoma: A Sharia advocate beheads a woman after calling for Islamic terror and posting an Islamist beheading photo.

June 2014, West Orange, New Jersey: A 19-year-old college student is shot to death 'in revenge' for Muslim deaths overseas.

June 2014, Seattle, Washington: Two homosexuals are murdered by an Islamic extremist.

April 2014, Skyway, Washington: A 30-year-old man is murdered by a Muslim fanatic.

Since 9/11, at the time of this writing, we have had nearly 72 attacks on U.S. soil in the name of Islam or in the name of ISIS. Another 30+ were stopped before they occurred.

Most of the attackers yelled "Praises to Allah" before committing these acts. Yet the incidences have been deemed everything from workplace violence to single acts of deranged people.

We can still buy ISIS flags and order ISIS-themed cakes. There is no resounding noise or uprising to ban the ISIS flag image like there was after the single shooting incident in Charleston, South Carolina.

RAMBLINGS

When Dylan Roof gunned down 9 black people in that Charleston church you would have thought from the subsequent media coverage that he was speaking for all people associated with the Confederate flag and that shootings associated with a Confederate flag were a regular occurrence that had to be stopped, NOW! He never yelled "long live the south" or "the south will rise again" or any other "racist" chant while doing so. Overwhelmingly, the American populous, including Southerners, denounced his actions. His only real connection to the Confederate flag was that he was pictured with it on social media. But it became the central focus. And the fallout from that ONE shooting continues with Civil War memorials being removed and soldiers being exhumed!

ONE racially motivated incident, by ONE deranged shooter who happened to be photographed with a Confederated battle flag, caused such furor that history is actively being rewritten right in front of our eyes.

Compare that to 65 attacks on US soil by Islamic extremists. Are there any calls to ban the flag? Nope. That ISIS flag is still easy to find here in the U.S. of A.

What is this double-standard? Why do some atrocities simply draw a gasp while others incite riots? And why do some groups always seems to get a pass?

I've come to the conclusion, if you are white and commit a crime using a gun you are tagged as a "right-wing, conservative, gun-loving, homophobic, bigoted racist" and represent everyone in the "white _____ " (fill in the blank) category.

But if you happen to be a "devoted Muslim, with beheading videos and ISIS propaganda all over your home and on your computer" and are even writing blogs to join the cause, you are a "lone wolf" with no ties to any other Muslim extremists. There's no pattern here.

A Lone Gunman Strikes?

There isn't enough booze or drugs to make that garbage make sense.

Speak out and speak up! Be the non-violent "Lone Wolf" and make a difference by speaking the truth.

Chapter 18

We don't need no stinkin military!

It's always been pretty obvious, for the most part, the Democrats have never been really fond of the military. If they had any feeling for them at all, I would say, based on the actions of many Dems that have taken up temporary residence in the White House, they loath them.

Whenever a Democrat gets in he (hasn't been a she yet) loves to whip out the red pen and get right to cutting the military budget and, in turn, taking a huge swipe at moral. They view enlisted as little more than "GI Joe" kids with low IQ's and no place else to go.

Don't believe me? How about we revisit some "terms of endearment" toward our military from our Democrat Leaders?

Democrat Rep. Jack Murtha has called our Marines, *"cold blooded killers."*

Democrat Senator John Kerry accused our soldiers of *"terrorizing women and children"* in Iraq.

Democrat Dick Durbin, the senior senator from Illinois, compared our military police at Guantanamo Bay to Nazis and Soviet gulag guards.

Democrat Senator Ted Kennedy once said that, *"Saddam's torture chambers reopened under new management, U.S. management."*

In 2008, the Democratic Chairwoman of the Virginia State Board of Election (appointed by the then-Democratic National Committee Chair Sen. Tim Kaine) argued that sending absentee ballots overseas to the military ONE day before the elections was perfectly legal. Really? What was the motivation? Why wouldn't we give these guys every chance to vote?

We don't need no stinkin military!

A federal court stepped in and ruled that Virginia violated federal law but conceded that without the original ballots there was no way to prove if the voting would have made a difference. So the moral to the Democrat voter story is to protect the votes of the dead, the illegals, and the non-existent, but to Hell with the military. We wouldn't want to go out of our way to accommodate them in any way!

Why, you ask? Because the majority of the military tends to vote Republican or conservative.

It's so very interesting that when Republicans fight to make sure every American citizen vote is protected, REAL citizens, by supporting voter ID laws, Democrats say Republican are trying to suppress the vote. In reality, the areas that have enacted voter ID laws show the voting numbers don't go down, they go up! In Georgia, voting among Black and Hispanics DRAMATICALLY increased from 2006 to 2012, outpacing the state's growth rate. How can that be? They have voter ID laws.

Yet Democrats actually sued to remove an exception giving the military voters an equal chance to be counted. When called out their response was, "We are only acting in the interest of fairness!" That can only work on the planet Uranus, you know, the one that spins backwards and off a normal axis!

Even Mr. Obama's warped sense of reality shone through when he said he supported gay marriage because of the soldiers "fighting on my behalf." He just doesn't support their right to vote. Gotta stop and think!

President Jimmy Carter decided, as did Mr. Obama, that America should seek peace through weakness. He cut military spending and overlooked many issues in the Middle East. He felt it was our strength that was causing tensions with Russia to the point of ordering his administration to dismantle 200 to 250 nuclear weapons on naval vessels in Europe and the Middle East. That worked out well.

He proposed cuts to operations and maintenance, reduced training and alert status equipment and more. This made our B-52 aircraft assigned to the Strategic Air Command at the lowest it had been since before the war. There was only 1/3 of the equipment needed to keep us safe. Why? Because he felt this would show the world we weren't bullies. Is this built into their DNA?

After President Reagan had left the most peace-keeping, combat-ready force on the planet, we had peace in the Middle East, had dismantled the Soviet empire, the respect of our allies, and a healthy fear from our enemies. In steps President Bill Clinton. He immediately went to work cutting the military and increasing the number of interns working at the White House. Bill cut the military by almost 30%. He let 500,000 military people go and allowed 80 ships to be mothballed without replacement. He cut

the military budget by $12 billion the first year and pushed to cut it by $88 billion by the end of his FIRST term.

Gen. Colin L. Powell, chairman of the Joint Chiefs of Staff, argued that the Administration's approach to our U.S. military was "fundamentally flawed" and the proposal was "out of balance." (Sound familiar?) There was a new plan to provide $400 million in expanded efforts to reduce the threat weapons of mass destruction "lost" or "misplaced" by the former Soviet Union.

We don't need no stinkin military!

Along with this proposal was a new $40 million dollar allocation to fund "counterproliferation measures" aimed at stopping the development of nuclear, chemical and biological weapons by such countries as North Korea, Iraq, and Iran. They were denied! HOW DID THAT WORK OUT?

Mr. Obama is following ALL of these same flawed ideas and adding some of his own! In watching a weekend special hosted by Bret Baier, three of President Obama's previous Defense Secretaries basically said the same thing: The President is wrong and dangerous on foreign policy. He is more interested in having a politically correct, totally socially-acceptable military than one that is fighting ready and feared!

~ ~

Instead of money for more training or equipment, we allocated money for our men on an ROTC event to walk around in high heels for the afternoon to see what it's like to be berated.

~ ~

The majority of his policies for the military have nothing to do with strengthening them, making them battle ready, or getting them better equipment. NO! It's about making sure that the LGBTQ community feels comfortable joining. It's about making sure that no one is offended by what's perceived to be racist or nasty language. It's about making sure that no one ever has to see any religious symbols (of the Christian type). But if you're a Sikh, then the head garb is ok. Or a Muslim, where special arrangements will be made for prayer daily. And the will be no pork in some of the major mess halls. But, I bet there is meat on Friday at those same mess halls. No problem insulting our Catholic friends.

RAMBLINGS

Instead of money for more training or equipment, we allocated money for our men on an ROTC event to walk around in high heels for the afternoon to see what it's like to be berated. This clown of a president has made the military a circus. This is according to his last three defense secretaries, NOT Joe Messina. No doubt we will soon find these guys in trouble with the IRS, military police, or worse, dead.

The show was very telling. If you took Mr. Obama's name off of it you would call the person a warped hater of America. But since his name is on it many will quietly go away and say nothing.

I will say, if these Secretaries of Defense are telling us the truth, this president will eventually be known as the president who tried to bring down America.

What sane person keeps shrinking his military with the world increasingly in turmoil? What sane person keeps cutting money from the military budget and increasing money to services for illegals and refugees? What sane person stops border patrol agents from doing their job, leaving our borders basically open and unchecked?

Draw your own conclusion. No sane person would do that!

Chapter 19

LAWS? What are THEY?

The Dictator is at it again. Mr. Obama really has a mental health issue. After nearly 8 years, he still hasn't figured out that he is not a "dictator," he is not a "king," he is not our "supreme leader nor grand imperial poohbah." Nope he is just the president of the republic known as the United States.

Either this "constitutional professor" doesn't understand it or doesn't think it applies to him. You see, he can't just whip out his pen every time he feels like issuing an edict and expect everyone is going to fall in line like good little Borg drones.

~ ~ ~ ~ ~ ~ ~ ~ ~ ~ ~ ~ ~ ~ ~ ~ ~ ~ ~ ~

Either this "constitutional professor" doesn't understand it or doesn't think it applies to him.

~ ~ ~ ~ ~ ~ ~ ~ ~ ~ ~ ~ ~ ~ ~ ~ ~ ~ ~ ~

He has been doing this since he arrived on the scene. With the Department of Education, Homeland Security, and the EPA, just to name a few. He has single-handedly put thousands out of work in the coal industry and created more part-time, underpaid jobs than any other president.

On Thursday evening, Mr. Obama decided (sure he did, not like it was planned, it just happened all of a sudden) that he was going to make it plain and order ALL public schools to open up all bathrooms to transgenders. With all that is going on in the world and across this country THIS is the thing at the top of the list? Less than 1% of the population identifies as transgender. We are losing hundreds of veterans every year because they can't get in to see a doctor and he signs a transgender order? Why doesn't he make it for private schools, private colleges, heck make it for all government restrooms in every state? Why? Because it's a political move, you know, like Benghazi.

He figures that there are enough Americans on his side on this one and that any opposition from Republicans will kill them in their respective races.

As usual, Mr. Oblamo, you are wrong again sir. With every one of these lame moves of yours, you awaken the sleeping giant in this country. The right-wing or moderate religious person that was willing to "live and let live" is now seeing that you and your kind are NOT willing to let them live. You want them to come in line with you or face the consequences.

Even Liberal Democrats are doing a double-take on this one. Many writing and asking what they can do to stop it. Vote Republican. Period. Stop the insanity, vote Republican.

This wonderful country of ours was founded on laws, founded on the Constitution, not every whim of the president. This president, especially, has decided that the Founding Fathers were all wrong, whereas he hasn't had a wrong idea his whole life!

Last May the Obama Administration threatened to withdraw special funding to pay for hospitals and doctors for impoverished citizens if the states in question do not comply. It was Florida, Tennessee, Texas, and Kansas. The departments that handle Medicare and Medicaid also sent a message mandating they expand Medicaid or lose federal funding for uncompensated medical services. In other words, money for uninsured people, mostly illegals!

The states sued and WON! The Supreme Court ruled, the federal government could NOT force states to comply with the ACA by holding back or threatening to hold back funds. PERIOD!

LAWS? What are THEY?

So what does Mr. Oblamo do? He does it again. He issues an edict to allow all transgender children to use the bathroom of their choice in all public schools across the country. Over the weekend, an estimated 19 states (so far) will join in a lawsuit against the government. This is a state rights issue, again!

And why didn't Mr. Obama include private schools? Because his kids go to a private school! And don't give me that "it's a private business, so he can't force them." He tried to force private institutions to give birth control against their beliefs now didn't he?

Mr. Obama's defenders and even Attorney General Loretta Lynch says it's a Title IX issue. REALLY? Pull her ticket! Nowhere does it infer or state that "transgender" is a protected class. I'm simply saying, the top law enforcer doesn't know the law.

HE continues to bypass congress, bypass the Constitution, and ignore the Supreme Court. That can only mean one thing. He sees himself as all-knowing, all-seeing, and perfect. Here's your tip for the day... Get out of the way before that lightning bolt hits!

Chapter 20

You CAN Trust the Government?

During the 2016 presidential primaries, we were pummeled with nothing but distractions. Trump is immoral, Rubio sold his home to a lobbyist, and Cruz is not a citizen. They had us chasing our tails like a cat chases a red laser dot on the wall!

Our government keeps telling us they have our best interests at heart, and will do what's best for us, and can keep us safe!

When a private company puts out a product that is supposed to be safe for us and it's found not to be, the government protects us by fining them, making them fix it, or shutting them down altogether.

Unless of course that company or entity is... The Government!

When the government, through another government agency, OK's a drug or procedure for use because the "government" has checked it out and deemed it safe for humans but then finds several years later it's not, they levy huge fines on that company, set up trust funds to accommodate the payouts, and line lawyer pockets so everyone is a winner! Right?

How about when they tell you certain foods are bad for you? Then a few years later they are suddenly good for you. Only to find out down the road that people are growing second heads, extra fingers, or feet from those same so-called "safe ingredients." You know, like the sawdust or wood content in your grated cheese. Stay with me here...

You CAN Trust the Government?

You see, our government keeps telling us these regulations and services are here to help us and when they fail they just keep adding more, like using chewing gum to plug holes in a dam.

BUT they fail at almost, note I said ALMOST, everything they do to "protect" us.

They spend hundreds of millions of dollars setting up online Obamacare exchanges that not only did not operate properly (even though they kept throwing millions at them to try to fix them) but come to find out, there was no real security on the backend to keep your medical data safe.

Do you know what happens to a hospital, doctor, or pharmacy who doesn't protect your medical or personal data? The government says, "The penalties for noncompliance are based on the level of negligence and can range from $100 to $50,000 per violation (or per record), with a maximum penalty of $1.5 million per year for violation(s)."

The government admitted they never checked security on the exchanges and hundreds of thousands of records were stolen. Who would you fine? Hmm? Each agency is funded with taxpayer dollars so the taxpayer would lose again. What a deal!

When Visa and MasterCard were hacked, the banks and institutions were fined millions of dollars and forced to implement tighter security. In reality, the fines were passed on to the consumers, but we signed up for it and we can leave at any time.

The government, in the form of the IRS, after spending millions of dollars for computer system upgrades and software security upgrades was hacked!

The IRS originally told us that a little over 300 thousand records had been hacked by _____ (fill in the blank). But in reality, over 700 thousand records were stolen. Think hard. Tax ID's, residences, assets, account numbers, and so on. Everything a thief would need to make your life a living hell!

~ ~

Over 700,000 records were stolen. Think hard. Tax ID's, residences, assets, account numbers, and so on. Everything a thief would need to make your life a living hell!

~ ~

Then there was that little issue with the CIA director's email being hacked by a 17-year-old. Let that sink in. He gained access to the home system by saying he was a Verizon employee. No one called Verizon to verify? At the home of the Chief of the CIA?! HELLO! But, sure, we can trust the government can keep us safe!

The NSA was informed by the Chinese government that their system was hacked by a group from their country, saying they were able to break in during a system upgrade.

Thousands of names, addresses, Social Security numbers, account info, health info, and more of government agents with high-end security clearances are now sitting on computer systems in China along with information about immediate family members, also hacked!

Isn't it good to know that the people who say they can protect us, our medical information, our banking information, our gun information, and so much more, actually CAN'T protect us?!

Doesn't all that make you feel safe?

When the government says, "We can protect you" you should get that comforting feeling you get when you hear the snap of the rubber glove right before a prostate exam!

America, protect yourself because The Government won't do it!

Chapter 21

Ignorance is now coveted

Have you heard about the implosion of socialism in Venezuela? Or should I say, the blow up of Venezuela because of socialism?

Food trucks being hijacked, black market food skyrocketing, a dozen eggs selling for over 100 bucks, toilet paper, milk, and other basic necessities not being provided or even available for the general public. YEP! In a socialist nation where everyone is equal. Equally BROKE!

Presidential candidate and Senator, Bernie Sanders said we should embrace socialism because it treats everyone fairly and provides for all. That must have been one heck of an acid trip Bern! The upper 1% get all the toilet paper, food, water, and electricity they want, while "The People" get what the government says they can have. And right now, in Venezuela, that isn't much.

Bernie was asked about socialism and why he thinks it's so great, especially since we are seeing the oil-producing, socialist country of Venezuela unravel before our eyes. And recently we've watched the failures of other socialist nations like Argentina, Brazil, Cuba, Haiti, Greece, and the European Union... all EPIC FAILURES! Bernie responded with, "I didn't come here to speak about socialism, I came here to speak about my campaign." The commentator said, "You are touting the virtues of socialism on your campaign trail." After a moment of silence Bernie said again, "I didn't come here to discuss that." A real winner in that one!

Russia is really operating under socialism and can't get out of their own way. It's is one of the richest countries on the planet in terms of natural resources. They are loaded with natural gas, diamonds, oil reserves, and great farm land but somehow the ability to feed its people or give them "fair and equitable" housing alludes them.

When asked about socialism, Liberal Loons respond pretty much the same way all the time basically saying, "go away," "you're stupid," and "fear-monger." They can't even string together a sentence with structure and substance. WHY? Because they got nuthin'! They don't know. They are ill-informed and the way to win (so they believe) is to brow-beat and insult, rather than actually deal with the issue.

~ ~

They are ill-informed and the way to win (so they believe) is to brow-beat and insult, rather than actually deal with the issue.

~ ~

My wife (also my producer and editor) Tammy recapped an on-air story I recently covered about socialism. When I scanned the reader comments I was floored! Not really. Nothing the far Left does really floors me anymore. One reader wrote:

> "How long did you spend in Venezuela? My students and family there would be really upset if they knew that a privileged [sic] lady like you is so misinformed about what a dictatorship looks like versus true DEMOCRACY."

First of all lady, we are comparing socialism to a REPUBLIC, not a democracy. Hello! Get a clue! Secondly, are you really that blind? Are you so afraid or prideful that you will have to concede that socialism works NOWHERE that you're willing to bury your head in a really dark place so you can ignore people eating their own pets and paying over 100 bucks for a dozen eggs? Food truck drivers are being beaten and the trucks hijacked. This isn't a joke.

87

Ignorance is now coveted

The government shut down government buildings 2 days a week to save electricity and money. Martial law had to be established to keep the peace. You could have been SHOT for stealing food. Some of you bleeding hearts don't want to prosecute people in this country for stealing food for their families when they are in need. But somehow you have no issue with what is going on in Venezuela? The Loon who commented thinks Venezuela is a true democracy? I want to know what she's smoking.

Socialism doesn't work, it never has. It takes so much away from individuals. Socialism doesn't allow for incentives to better oneself or move up. The economy is not market driven. Property is owned by the state and they decide who gets what and when. With no incentives, there's no reason to work harder. There's no real hope that you can achieve your goals and happiness. Under socialism, collective ownership is what's important, not individual achievement.

China, though using a more "capitalistic approach" to their financial markets, still adheres to strong socialist values, except for the top one percent. Many companies in China are owned by the government or friends of the government. From a young age you're groomed to understand the government knows best about everything. They choose what career you will have, where you will live, and how much you will be paid. Sounds like paradise, doesn't it?! No thanks!

RAMBLINGS

Watch the interviews of the "Bernie Millennials." They are strong advocates for socialism because the government pays for education, housing, food, medical, and more. Sounds like prison to me! They think that the government will share the resources so everyone is treated equally. Think again.

The government has NEVER done a good job of taking from the rich and giving to the poor. They have done a great job of taking from the hard working, and taking from the hard working, and taking from the hard working (no I didn't stutter) and trickling a small portion of what's left, what they didn't waste, to people in need. But they've yet to work on a solution as to how to get them off government aid. Just ways for getting more government aid.

Millennials think that helping people is socialism, but it's not. Helping people is actually accomplished through capitalism. Private organizations do a much better job at helping out non-profits who then actually distribute more of the resources (private money) out to the people in need. It's private money that funds much of the research and development for breakthroughs in medicine and science as well as new energy sources and new technologies. Very few innovations come out of socialist and communist countries. Period.

Capitalism is the only way for individuals and countries to pull themselves out of poverty and eventually be able to help other people and, in turn, other nations take care of their own.

Watching the Bernie millennials, I now understand that saying from years gone by... "Youth is wasted on the young."

Chapter 22

No such thing as Mainstream Christianity!

Words have meaning right? Society keeps "evolving" with words or, in reality, the left just changes the meanings to suit the political atmosphere.

This used to be something only hardcore politicos might attempt but I'm finding more and more of "mainstream" Christians are now doing the same thing. Some Christians find it necessary to dance around or water down the true meanings of God's Word and commandments just so people around them won't think they are too harsh or "religious."

Why is that? What would cause someone who says they believe in something to change it or ignore parts of it to make themselves feel better?

Now, it's not my intention to disrespect my Catholic friends, but U.S. Representative Nancy Pelosi is, in her own words, a "devout Catholic." How can that be?

Mainstream Catholic churches believe the Pope is the supreme leader and the final word on earth for interpreting the meaning of scripture. It's based on the Catholic understanding that Peter was the first Pope by way of Christ saying He would build his church on the truth that Peter spoke when Christ asked him who He was.

How about a couple of examples: You can't follow Muhammad and say you're a Christian! You can't make Christ your Lord and be a Buddhist. You can't be a smoker and never touch a cigarette (or whatever your smoke of choice is).

Pelosi says she is a devout Catholic, however she believes in abortion. The Church and scripture are against abortion. Nancy is an advocate of same-sex marriage, however the Catholic Church is opposed to same-sex marriage. So, what Catholic Church or doctrine is she really following?

Not long ago, I had words with someone on Facebook about a Christian issue. At first I thought I was discussing the Bible with a follower of Christ. After a bit, I wasn't so sure. Now for the record, there's no way for me to know if this person is a follower of Christ, that's not for me to decide. That issue is between them and Christ. But the Bible does say we would know them by their fruits and how we treat each other Christian to Christian.

What started the conversation was that she wrote about how proud she was that her son wrote a play/poem based on the story of Adam and Eve. But he added a reference to "Steve." He took a different viewpoint from what scripture said and had a different viewpoint of what Eve or Adam was thinking and doing. When I questioned her, she said the story was basically a fairy tale. She in a few paragraphs stated that most of the stories in the Bible were not real, but simply stories written by men.

Now I am already confused and we hadn't even gotten into it yet. You see, MOST Christians believe the Bible is the Word of God written down as the Spirit of God gave it to man to write.

She states she is a Christian, but she doesn't take the Bible at face value because it was written by men. She said that she follows what's written in red (denotes the words of Christ) but notes that the Bible is a guideline not a commandment on how to live your life. Now I'm really confused.

If the Bible is written by men and can't be trusted, then how did she know her faith in Christ is real? I mean, that part was written by men too. NEWSFLASH! The red parts were also written by men. Uh oh!

The Bible is very clear in several places that it's the guideline for life as a Christian. It's God's will (our manual) for our life. Yes, we can choose to ignore it or choose to use it. It also tells us to study and not just read. It's not a novel, but a workbook!

The Christian church has allowed many negative things to creep into the church. And the church, as a whole, has largely ignored its responsibilities, partly because Christians refuse to study and live out their lives according to scripture.

I am not advocating we fight each other from within, but we should not allow all the lies to infiltrate our lives. The Bible is clear about protecting what you see, hear, and allow into your heart and head.

To my Christian friends... Our kids are suffering because we don't live out our faith according to God's Word. God's Word is absolute on so many things and we have not conveyed that to our children. Our "anything goes" society is setting the values for your children via sex education at school and the TV shows they watch, among other things being thrown at them.

~ ~

"YOU call certain things abominations because you find them icky." No. I called them that because the Bible says they are and the Bible is God's Word.

~ ~

The woman on Facebook was upset that I chose to use the scripture that says that a man using the body of another man as a woman is an abomination to God. She said *"YOU call certain things abominations because you find them icky."* No. I called them that because the Bible says they are and the Bible is God's Word. As a Christian why wouldn't I say it?

So again I ask, if you're a Christian, why are you a Christian? Because you go to church? Because your grandma went to church? Or because you follow the teachings of Jesus Christ?

RAMBLINGS

There are many things Jesus says to do that may be uncomfortable. Christians should not shy away from those things.

What I find is that they sometimes make teenage excuses for not following the Bible. *"Well that book is 2000 years old. It doesn't pertain to us today."* Sure it doesn't! *"Religion is a personal thing. It should be kept to yourself."* Yup, it was really personal for Christ when He was beaten in public, carried His cross in public, was embarrassed on the cross in public, and then publically forgave all those who came against Him in public. Yup, sounds like a very private thing to me... NOT!

If you don't believe it all, then how do you know that Christ is the way? It's the only book, written by men, that says HE is!

My point with all this is aimed at my true brothers and sisters in Christ. Time for a checkup. Take an inventory of your life. Does it match up to the Word? When someone says something wrong about God does it bother you as much as someone saying someone nasty against your Mom, your wife, your husband, or your children?

Some of you write me and say, *"Joe, where's the love of Christ? God calls us to love everyone."* Yup, and He also calls us to hate evil. "Love" is the most overused word in our language. Did Jesus love the Pharisees and Sadducees when he called them vipers? When He told the adulteress to go and sin no more (which implies what she was doing was a sin) was He showing her love? He openly accused her of sinning and doing something wrong. He did not ACCEPT her behavior. Did that mean He did not love her? Of course not. When you grounded your son or daughter for lying to you, or cheating on a test, or whatever, did you not love them in that moment? No. It's because of your love that you do those things.

No such thing as Mainstream Christianity!

I'm not telling you to run around and stick your finger in people's faces telling them they're sinning and going to hell. What I'm telling you is, don't accept things that are against God's Word or allow them to enter your life. You have control. You are setting an example to your kids and others around you.

You only need to care about what God thinks of you. Don't worry about the rest.

Chapter 23

There's a bottom to the bucket?

If any of you have taken Dave Ramsey's financial classes you know he uses an "envelope system" to help you budget and save money. You can easily see where money is being spent, how it's growing, or dwindling, and so on.

The government can't make envelopes that big, so we talk in terms of buckets. Based on the way they spend money, it's obvious they don't just think we have buckets full, we must have skip loaders full!

We all know about the basic "buckets"...

Military, health and welfare, education, and a few others. For those of you who really don't get it, the government does not make "revenue," they collect taxes. Or in plain, simple English, they take your money!

I don't have a real problem paying taxes. I don't want to do it, but I do understand the need to pay taxes for the basics like first responders (fire, police, ambulance), military, "basic" healthcare (hospitals and clinics), road work and maintenance (in the form of tire or gas taxes), snow removal, landslide removal, you get the picture. Paying basic taxes for services received.

But, I don't want to fund the government's stupidity and inability to spend money wisely. Enter the Progressive Left. Who made the noise when we were paying $90 for a toilet seat and $300 for hammers? (Republicans.) When we paid that EPA employee for 8 years who never showed up for work? (Republicans.) And what about the millions of dollars in new buildings for government workers when we have numerous empty ones that we aren't even renting out or selling? (Republicans.) When can I scream for you to simply stop wasting money?

I keep hearing from the Left how the "rich" can afford to pay more, when, in reality, they are already paying more percentage-wise of their income than the 99%-ers. Why? They made better decisions, took greater risk, and, therefore, made more money. Guess what? A majority of those "rich people" are Democrats!

Democrats keep saying rich people should pay more taxes, but where is their money? The Dems have some of the richest congressmen on The Hill (they don't all arrive rich, but most leave rich!) They keep talking about closing tax loopholes, but what bill have Democrats put on the table that would have closed the loopholes that they themselves take advantage of? None!

Mr. Obama continues to tell us all the good things he and the Liberal Democrats have done and how everything is going to be rainbows and butterflies. Unemployment is still abysmal and we still have fewer full-time workers today than when he took office! We have less worker participation than when he took office. There's not enough money in the unemployment and disability buckets (now being funded by these new part-time taxpayers). They'll say the government is paying the shortage, but we are the government, so taxpayers are paying for it!

~ ~

Mr. Obama continues to tell us all the good things he and the Liberal Democrats have done and how everything is going to be rainbows and butterflies.

~ ~

He tells us how families can now afford health insurance thanks to the Affordable Care Act, and for the first time in history many families have insurance who couldn't get it before! Another program carried on the backs of the taxpayer through the HHS tax bucket. Many of these policies are subsidized by the government, sorry, I mean taxpayers... Many families lost their health insurance and had to go to a substandard health policy with longer wait periods and longer drives for people to see their doctors and get help. Additionally, they now have larger deductibles. Remember how he said that it would "cost you less than the average cell phone bill" but then switched to "you will need to tighten your budget and cut out some things you don't have to have." Instead of saving the average family $2500 a year, it's ended up costing the average family about $10,473 a year. That's from Forbes (2015), not TRS!

He continues to tell us that families can get ahead, realize the American dream, and own a home. In reality, home ownership is down from when he took office by 3%, median income is down, many people working part-time instead of full-time jobs, the poverty level has increased, and people on food stamps have almost doubled. These government subsidized programs are paid from the welfare bucket! Apparently, in the President's world, having less somehow translates into a better chance of realizing the American dream!

He boasts that gas is at an all-time low (as if he deliberately had a hand in making it happen). I doubt he'll issue a big "shout out" and "thank you" to ISIS. If you want to thank Obama for this I suppose you can. His inactivity in squelching the "JV team" known as ISIS has allowed them to steal millions of gallons of oil, ship it in stolen tankers, and sell the oil at prices that make the Saudi Arabians look bad. The Saudis then dropped prices to match so that they could stay in the game and drive the price of a barrel of gas so low that the American oil companies couldn't afford to produce and would therefore shut down local refineries. Congratulations, even more people on unemployment. The welfare and unemployment buckets are going to need more taxpayer money.

Several economists have said that even if we took 90% of the money from the country's richest people and richest corporations, it wouldn't make a double-digit dent in America's woes. All it would do is make the lower 99% feel better because you dinged the rich guys.

How many of you get most or all of your income tax money back? We have more people than ever on food stamps, welfare, and assisted medical, and they're talking about wiping out school loans and giving

There's a bottom to the bucket?

free college educations. And don't get me started on illegal immigrant benefits! No money in, lots of money out. It's sheer lunacy!

We can't keep it up. The buckets are empty and no one cares! There is a bottom to the bucket and when we finally find it, America will be in a world of hurt!

Chapter 24

We are Guaranteed Freedom of Nothing!

In July of 2015 we celebrated over 230 years of protection from the United States Army. These brave men and women have been dying for our freedom to be stupid for a long time.

I am enraged by the Obama Administration's continued attacks on the military and even more so by the Administration's inability to allow these men and woman to live out their belief systems. If there is a war on women that has been started by the Republicans, then the war on God has been started by, fueled by, and actively pursued by the Democrats.

Now Democrats, before you get all uppity on me, remember, some of you have no problem blaming all Republicans for the bad decisions a Republican president and his staff made, so you need to swallow and own your own playbook. The

Democrats own the White House and, therefore, all the tomfoolery coming out of it. This president, who says he is for freedom of religion, seems to never stop living in "backwards day."

This Administration has strongly objected to an amendment to the National Defense Authorization Act that would simply allow freedom of religious speech for soldiers. The amendment was authored by Rep. John Fleming, R-LA. It would have:

"required the Armed Forces to accommodate 'actions and speech' reflecting the conscience, moral, principles or religious beliefs of the member."

This is a blatant attack on Christianity. How so, you ask? Accommodations are still made for the prayer rituals of Muslims. 5 times a day! Special rooms, approved absences in the middle of shifts, and so on.

The new rules being put in place by the administration would require soldiers to keep Bibles out of plain view. If soldiers are sitting on their bunks discussing the Bible, God, or Jesus and a non-believing soldier walks in and is offended they have to stop! Chaplains performing services can't use the name of Jesus, even if the family asks.

My favorite saying as of late is that the world must be spinning in the opposite direction.

~ ~ ~ ~ ~ ~ ~ ~ ~ ~ ~ ~ ~ ~ ~ ~ ~ ~ ~ ~

Here in the good ol' U.S. of A. intolerance towards religion is encouraged, especially against those that are Christ-centered or hold an "unfavorable" viewpoint toward gay marriage, illegal immigration, and waiting to have sex before marriage. We are so screwed as a society.

~ ~ ~ ~ ~ ~ ~ ~ ~ ~ ~ ~ ~ ~ ~ ~ ~ ~ ~ ~

Comrade Putin has declared in mother Russia that no hate speech towards churches or religions will be tolerated. Unlike the U.S., violations in Russia are publishable by imprisonment. Here in the good ol' U.S. of A. intolerance towards religion is encouraged, especially against those that are Christ-centered or hold an "unfavorable" viewpoint toward gay marriage, illegal immigration, and waiting to have sex before marriage. We are so screwed as a society.

RAMBLINGS

Regarding the military: The current Administration needs to get its head out of the very dark, odorful place it has had it in for many years and get back to reality. Anyone willing to fight for my freedom, take a bullet for me or my family, in simple words for the overeducated, anyone willing to die fighting for me, should be able to have and speak of any God, scripture, and belief system they want. If a soldier wants to "Hail Satan," then so be it.

There have been virtually no complaints by non-believing enlisted soldiers. The complaints come primarily from attorneys and organizations... cowards. These people aren't on the front lines. They are not fighting. And they typically have no relationship with our soldiers or their families. They're cowards.

President Obama, get a grip on reality. I know you have no use for our military except as doormen and umbrella holders, but they have more courage, integrity, and love for our county and its people in their baby finger than you have had your whole life.

Do you doubt this is really happening? Author Todd Starnes reported via RedState.com just a few examples of Christian service members and chaplains whose 1st Amendment right to religious freedom was silenced:

- The Air Force censored a video created by a chaplain because it included the word "God." The Air Force feared the word might offend Muslims and atheists.

- A service member received a "severe and possibly career-ending reprimand" for expressing his faith's religious position about homosexuality in a personal religious blog.

- A senior military official at Fort Campbell sent out a lengthy email officially instructing officers to recognize "the religious right in America" as a "domestic hate group" akin to the KKK and Neo-Nazis because of its opposition to homosexual behavior.

We are Guaranteed Freedom of Nothing!

- A chaplain was relieved of his command over a military chapel because, consistent with DOMA's definition of marriage (at the time), he could not allow same-sex weddings to take place in the chapel.

For the record I blame my "religious" brothers for the loss of these freedoms. We allowed this to happen. We never wanted to make waves because we were afraid that we might offend someone. These are the consequences of inaction. Slowly but surely we are losing our freedom to speak openly about our religious beliefs. I, for one, will not go down easily. Will you?

Chapter 25

It's not a Women's Health Issue!

I have been saying, to the irritant of my friends on the Left, that abortion has nothing to do with women's health.

One of the original questions the Supreme Court had to deal with in the seventies when they approved this "slaughter law" was, when does life begin. Well, all the academics and doctors who were willing to take some money and testify said life did not start until the third trimester.

Remember, this was a time when cancer was almost always fatal, AIDS was a death sentence, and, in some cases, people still died from the flu.

Medicine has come a long way since then. And now, many agree, scientists and doctors alike, that life begins at conception or shortly thereafter.

Dr. Bill Fifer, a professor of psychiatry at Columbia University, said,

> *"Everything that a newborn baby does, a fetus has pretty much done already."* He went on to say *"We know that a baby's tiny heart is beating as early as 18 days after sperm-egg fusion. Brain waves are detectable by 6 weeks and babies can experience dream (REM) sleep by 17 weeks. Substantial medical and scientific evidence has demonstrated that unborn children are capable of feeling pain by 20 weeks, if not earlier."*

Not Joe Messina's opinion, but science. This is now the understanding of many in the medical field. However, I am still perplexed. You see, the Left continually beats on Right-wing, conservative, Bible-thumping Republicans (like myself) for not believing in science but rather the fairy tales of the Bible.

But when confronted by science and facts (not theories like, let's say, evolution) that don't line up with their way of thinking they ignore them and tell us that we hate women (in the case of our abortion stance.) Why? Because it's easier than discussing the facts.

So, if at 18 days that little blob of cells has a heartbeat, what can we call it? What will it eventually be? A canine? A fish? A tree? Nope. Simply, a human. Its only potential outcome is that it is a developing human!

Now with science we can see with sonograms and 3-D imagery what the baby looks like. We can't run from that truth. Our youth are seeing it more and more and are changing the way they view abortion.

So then... it is a life! But what about the argument for years from the Left and the pro-abortion groups that it's not a life? As of late, some of the abortion proponents are saying that life begins when the mother says it does, that the unborn blob of cells can be snuffed out even up to the time it's exiting the birth canal. Wow! That's a stretch!

But wait! Jodi Jacobson, Editor in Chief of RH Reality Check, a Reproductive and Sexual Health and Justice blog says it was never when life beings because *"life begins at conception."* Huh?

OMG! Wasn't the abortion debate all about women having access to clean safe medical facilities so that when they were seeking this "medical procedure" the mother's health would not be at risk? The fetus, or as it's been called "blob of cells," needed to be removed to save the mother.

You were duped! Like all things Democrat, there were chapters and chapters between the lines that they hid from you!

According to Ms. Jacobson, this has always been a right to give a woman total control over her body! Well, one thing we can agree on, women should have control of their own bodies. Yes, she should definitely control it. If she doesn't want a baby, then she should keep her clothes on. If she can't do that, then at least have protected sex. And if she can't do that, well then, what kind of control does she really have over her body anyway?

~ ~

Well, one thing we can agree on, women should have control of their own bodies. Yes, she should definitely control it. If she doesn't want a baby, then she should keep her clothes on. If she can't do that, then at least have protected sex. And if she can't do that, well then, what kind of control does she really have over her body anyway?

~ ~

We have come to that point in society where life has no value. If you believe in science then the baby exists at a minimum within the first 20 days. What makes that life less valuable than the mother's life? Because the mother says so? Talk about playing God!

Now understand, even to the irritation of my Christian friends, I am pro-choice but ANTI-abortion. I believe God gave us choice, so who am I to take it away? God allows you to love or to hate. Love your kids or abuse your kids. Kill or give life. Lie or tell the truth. Help others or help no one. It's your choice. So, to my

It's not a Women's Health Issue!

Christian friends, the law changes nothing. God saw that His people weren't abiding by the 10 Commandments He gave them, so He sent Jesus with 2 simpler ones and they work just fine.

When it comes to the abortion debate, it boils down to this. People want what they want and they don't want to be told what to do. Ladies, if it's all about you wanting to control your bodies then control it! When you lose control don't tag us with the cost of your abortion or contraception pills or the medical and mental treatment you may need because of what you did. Why do we have to pay for your inability to control something you have forced us to allow you to choose?

Be an adult. Be responsible. There are 35 couples waiting for every 1 baby put up for adoption in this country! Over half of all pregnancies in the U.S. are unintended. Really? Are condoms not available in some parts of this country? From what I can see, they are at every gas station.

Even though abortion is actually on the decrease, they are up among poorer Americans, mostly the black community (Margaret Sanger must be very proud). Four of every 10 pregnancies end in abortion. Nine out of 10 abortions happen within the first 12 weeks (when the heart is beating and many of the "human" functions are forming). 56% of them are unmarried and 70 percent say they have a religious affiliation (though I don't know which one).

I have said all that to say... We were lied to. If this was really a women's health issue, then prove it! Currently, the fights are about abortion on demand for just about any reason and that now includes gender and race selection. Yep, you read that right... race!

Does life have value or not? Is one life worth more than another? Says who? And why do you get to play God?

Chapter 26

Is the Government your God?

When I was a child we were told to work hard, be honest, do your best, stand out, run faster, push, push, push. That's how you got ahead. That is so old school!

No, no Johnny, don't strain yourself, come over here grab this Xbox controller and relax. Johnny, put that homework away. You look stressed. Grab this Gameboy and blow off some steam. We aren't pushing our kids to do anything.

Back in the early eighties the "psychobabologists" (experts in "psycho-babble," yes, I know it's not really a word!) got together and decided that we were tearing down our young people's self-esteem by grading them and having winners and losers in sports. According to a University of Michigan study, grading a student was "degrading" because the student based their worth on their grades. I say, humbug!

The study went on to say that low self-esteem led to poor health and potentially more involvement in criminal behavior. They go on to say that bad grades are usually attributed to poor communities. But do grades cause low self-esteem which then has a domino effect?

Kids from all walks of life get bad grades, behave badly in school, and so on. But for now, let's discuss what these "psychobabologists" are selling... grades degrade kids.

Most wealthy people who came up from "the hood" got out by working harder, getting a better education, getting off the streets, and aspiring to be something other than a street hoodlum.

Those who work harder and have better grades tend to get into college easier and for less money (through grants and scholarships). Why? Does it mean they are worth more? No. It means they worked harder, wanted more for themselves, had a vision, and were willing to push toward it to get the grades needed to get out of their situation.

On the Liberal side of the fence, Whoopi Goldberg tells her story of sleeping in her car with her kids and on welfare. She wanted more. Does that make her a bad person? No. She made it out of her situation! Good for her!

On the Conservative side, there's Star Parker with a very similar story. She, too, came out of it.

Both were black, single females on welfare that wanted a better life for themselves and their children. They were willing to work hard to achieve it. They used the tools available to them, got ahead, and got off the government support system. God bless them both!

Both are great examples of what America is meant to be. It doesn't seem that either of them have any self-esteem or self-worth issues. And I bet both of them received grades!

And then there's the criticism of keeping score, and now recommendations that there should be no scorekeeping. Scorekeeping is bad. It makes the kids feel bad about themselves when they lose. Seriously? According to the "psychobabologists"!

I suppose this also means we should get rid of professional sports, the Olympics, and academic decathlons? Why would we, as enlightened human beings, want to make so many people feel so badly about themselves, to the point of lowering their self-esteem and self-worth, thereby making them sick and causing them to pursue a life of crime? That is the inference that's being made. Crazy, huh?

Major inventions and successful businesses, too numerous to mention, have followed failure, or someone else beating them to market with a product. Those losses are what make us stronger, better, and more caring people. Making everyone the same breeds mediocrity. No scores, no winners or losers, no grades. Why bother?

~ ~

Making everyone the same breeds mediocrity. No scores, no winners or losers, no grades. Why bother?

~ ~

A 2001 Sports Illustrated study showed that a large portion of children who started playing organized sports by age 6 usually quit by age 13 because they were no longer having any "fun." There is a lesson here that we are losing in America. How badly do you want it?

This is a great lesson for children. Tell Little Johnny and Little Suzie that competition is not always fun. Competition can be painful and disappointing. Getting to the top is not always fun and it's not easy. But when you get there and you look back at all the hard work you can say "I did it," "I built it" (not the government), and "it was worth it."

Low self-esteem isn't avoided by an absence of failure. Real self-esteem is earned by recovering from and overcoming failures (and encouragement from family and friends helps too!) You learn that you really can do it if you don't give up. And when others look at you and know what you've been through to get where you are, your story can give them hope that they, too, can do what you have done.

Chapter 27

The "N-Word" has a clone!

An elementary school principal was suspended for using the N-word. Well, she kind-of used the N-word. In a nutshell, the teacher was getting the kids ready for a play about Martin Luther King, Jr. After using the word "Negro" several times, one of the children said he was uncomfortable with that word and refused to participate in the play.

Ultimately the principal was called in for backup, and during the course of explaining the differences between the two N-words, "Negro" and "Ni***r", ended up getting herself in trouble. She has been suspended pending an investigation. But why?

I am at a loss here, to a degree. The word "Negro" has been an acceptable "descriptor" for many years. I have had not a one black friend tell me that was a bad word. It's the Spanish word for black. Martin Luther King, Jr. used the word several times in speeches to help explain or add understanding.

But when the principal used the OTHER N-word, well, I'm not going to judge her attempted explanation. It isn't available for us to critique. But if it went something like this, is this really a problem:

> *"Now, some people use the word Negro and some use the terribly, derogatory word NI***R. That second word is a word you should never call or refer to someone as. It's a hateful word and has no place in society. It was used in a hateful and mean way in this country in at a time when slavery was practiced. It was used to try to make black people feel like less of a person, sub-human even. It wasn't right then, and it isn't right now, EVER!"*

I need help here. Educators have asked that the "Ni***r" word be removed from Huckleberry Fin and Tom Sawyer, but, if we don't remind ourselves of the hate that was taught at a period of time in this country, how do we avoid it again in the future?

Have the word police gone too far? So many terms and words have become taboo. But why? I am not suggesting all words are OK to use in general conversation. What I am saying is that we have gotten so concerned with hurting someone's feelings and how they perceive us that we want our kids to avoid unpleasant things.

~ ~ ~ ~ ~ ~ ~ ~ ~ ~ ~ ~ ~ ~ ~ ~ ~ ~ ~ ~

Our youth need to have that same feeling. These words aren't cool. They're cruel and they need to know that.

~ ~ ~ ~ ~ ~ ~ ~ ~ ~ ~ ~ ~ ~ ~ ~ ~ ~ ~ ~

I am an American of Italian decent. My grandparents spoke and wrote Italian. It was their first language as was my mom's. When my mom moved me to a "white" neighborhood so I could have a better life I was called all kinds of colorful names, "dumb Dago," "Wop," "Guinea," and "Greaseball." (Sorry if that offends, but it really is what they called me!) Did they make me feel good? No. Did I think it was no big deal? No! Do I want them taken out of references in today's literature and books? No!

Let's get one thing straight. I am not comparing my school experience with slavery. I am comparing hurtful words. I want a generation 100 years from today to know how Italians, Japanese, Irish, blacks, and others were beaten down with words. I want them to read about it in books, on tablets, via text, and Tweets so they can see, and maybe feel, for themselves how distasteful it is and was and will continue to be, so they don't do it.

Think of all the horrible things that have happened in history. The Holocaust has gone from a full chapter in many history books to a page or a few paragraphs. How do our kids learn and understand the impact in that short account? The Japanese internment camps that were here, in this country, are down to a bare mention because they are distasteful and uncomfortable for our young kids. The history of slavery and the way we treated black people in this country is also being taught less and less.

History, no matter how uncomfortable, needs to be taught. Our kids and their kids need to know the mistakes of the past to ensure they don't repeat them in the future.

When I hear the word "Ni***r" spoken, whether from a black to a black or someone trying to start a fight or even just be funny, I cringe, not out of fear but because I know what that word represents. It isn't funny. It's hate. Plain and simple.

Our youth need to have that same feeling. These words aren't cool. They're cruel and they need to know that.

Chapter 28

It's Black, White, and Blue!

Mid 2016 was a very tough time for law enforcement officials that caused them to be on high alert ALL across the country.

That's the last thing we need for the men and women who protect us... all of us, no matter what color, what size, what religion, what dress, or what sexual orientation we are. When it comes to 99.9% of them, they just don't care about any of that. People are people and those officers are here for all of us. However, like any other profession, there are a few bad apples in every group.

There are almost 1 million law enforcement officials in this country. At any given point in time, there are almost 600 thousand on the streets of America. If what the Left-types like Texas' U.S. Congresswoman Sheila Jackson Lee have said is true, that *"Black boys are hunted down and killed like animals,"* then where is all the carnage? All those white, Bible-thumping, Conservative, Republican haters who own guns would be out hunting black kids for sport, right? Sound crazy? That's because IT IS!

After the Dallas police shootings, black female "Conservative" Kira Davis (I mention that as a disclaimer because I know some of you give no credibility to black Americans who are Conservative) said it's a real shame that we can't have an open, honest conversation about this.

Well, she's right... and wrong. We can't have the conversation because the Left gets nasty-nasty when you throw facts at them. We can't because if I, or any other white person, ask questions or suggests that committing less crimes, getting on the ground when instructed by an officer, or anything else that might shift blame makes us a racist or hater. BUT guess what? The Left, in stealing words' meanings, has made them of no effect!

The hard-Left, label-hating Loons have labeled everyone who does not agree with them as "phobic," "haters," "racists," and "bigots." That makes having an open and civil conversation kind of hard.

Here's a couple of facts. You can find them on your own. Check out FBI statistics and local law enforcement numbers. DO SOME WORK!

It's Black, White, and Blue!

52% of all murders are committed by blacks.
Blacks only make up 13% of the American population.

Now do you think 13% of a certain group in the population committing over half of the murders somehow makes the police at fault? Or racism at fault? Some of you right now are calling me a racist or picking up the phone calling stations telling them to drop me or telling web sites to stop carrying my column. For what? For speaking the truth? What, now a white guy can't state real statistics about the black community? If I do, it makes me racist. But if a black guy says the same numbers it's OK?

Chicago had over 2100 shootings in the first half of 2016. Over 370 are dead. THREE HUNDRED AND SEVENTY. These are almost ALL black-on-black crimes in black neighborhoods. Mr. Sharpton, Mr. Jackson, Mr. Obama any thoughts? No, this optic is not "sexy" enough and there's certainly not enough money in it!

Sweet Jesus, when are you all gonna wake up and help each other out? Stand up for each other. Take back your neighborhoods! Killing cops, burning down neighborhoods, shutting down freeways does absolutely nothing for you, NOTHING!

Mr. Sharpton, Mr. Jackson, and Mr. Obama, why aren't you there speaking out against it every day until it stops? Mr. Obama, instead of having a "beer summit" or jumping in on the Michael Brown case before all of the facts were in (you were wrong, it wasn't hands up don't shoot!) or talking

about how racism abounds in police departments while standing in front of the picture of 5 dead, white cops and their families, do something constructive to help these communities that are imploding.

Your distain for any authority but your own astounds us. Even those in your own party are taking notice.

Instead of speaking against the police most of the time, why aren't you there speaking out against a community who is killing their own? That "certain" group that was excited to have you in office because you were their color and were going to help them out. It's interesting that they are in worse shape today than they were 8 years ago.

After a shooting like the one in Orlando at the gay nightclub, I received many nasty emails telling me that because of my commentary on social issues I have blood on my hands. Simply because I don't agree with certain lifestyles and I don't believe in abortion, that whenever someone in the LGBTQ community gets hurt or killed it's my fault. When a woman dies from a botched abortion it's my fault. There was even one far-Left Loon who wrote telling me that after a 2-year-old girl was raped to death it was specifically my fault because I had done several stories about illegal refugees who were committing crimes, specifically, raping young toddlers and killing them.

~ ~ ~ ~ ~ ~ ~ ~ ~ ~ ~ ~ ~ ~ ~ ~ ~ ~ ~ ~

Do you think 13% of a certain group in the population committing over half of the murders somehow makes the police at fault? Or racism at fault?

~ ~ ~ ~ ~ ~ ~ ~ ~ ~ ~ ~ ~ ~ ~ ~ ~ ~ ~ ~

Well then, if I follow that logic, your messiah Mr. Obama, has blood on his hands. Mr. Obama you have many in your community that look up to you, who see you as a god, a role model, and as always correct.

When looking for the numbers of cops shot in the line of duty, many sites said it was on the decline. I'll let you guess who controlled those sites. So I decided to use the FBI source... 2014 spiked to 51 up 89% from the year before. One paper wrote that 2015 cop killing was down by 14%. WOW! One year of decline is now a trend? By June 2016, we were already up by 44% over last year and we were only half way through the year. By the last Saturday in June, we were up over 30 and 12 of these were ambushes. This is not acceptable. NOT AT ALL.

Mr. Obama came out and in one of the shortest speeches he's ever given said that these attacks on our law enforcement have to stop. They are the men and women who protect us. Great... What are you going to do to make that happen? Are you going to stop having the Black Lives Matter (BLM) people at the White House and stop telling them what great jobs their doing? Give up one golf game a week and visit an inner city that needs help? Go on a weekend. Show them what a great community organizer you were.

Mr. Obama, if you don't ratchet up your support for the police and call for your "leaders," the Sharpton's and the Jackson's of the world, to go out and denounce the violence then shame on you!

As the leader of the free world and America, the place you say you love, as the person you say has brought peace to the Middle East, repaired our international relationships, has ISIS on the run, has healed our economy, and fixed our middle America problem, why don't you use some of that magic to get the cop killers on the run, and give them a reason to stop killing our protectors?!

I forever #BackTheBlue. Blue Lives Matter, as do ALL lives! God bless our men and women in blue.

Chapter 29

Lying & Cheating & Stealing, OH MY!

I've been speaking with a lot of my not-so-political friends on the other side of the aisle. These are people who are usually very sensible. We find ourselves very close on issues, though we may take a different approach to get to the same conclusion, but sensible nonetheless.

During the primaries several of them expressed that they think Hillary may be best-suited for the presidency. The reason? She understands politics and has been at it longer than anyone else... all together now... SIGH!

But what's even more disturbing? The ones I considered politically sensible say that Hillary's issues really don't bother them because ALL politicians lie, ALL politicians cheat, and ALL have some issues that we don't know about. As if that weren't bad enough, some of those I spoke with were, wait for it... POLITICIANS! How sad! Have we become desensitized to bad actions and criminal behavior?

We turn a blind eye to some bad actions, but we keep passing ridiculous laws, like;

> *"You can only throw a Frisbee on a Los Angeles beach with a lifeguard's permission"* or
>
> *"Animals are banned from mating publicly within 1,500 feet of a tavern, school, or place of worship"* or this gem,
>
> *"No vehicle without a driver may exceed 60 miles per hour."*

Get my drift?

Over the years I have watched the American people and the legal system back down on truly criminal issues because we have too many people in jail. They say our judicial system is overloaded and can't take anymore. So now we stop enforcing laws or shorten jail sentences? We basically give up? Are we afraid to call them out as bad actions? Has political correctness made it wrong to call thugs, thugs; terrorists, terrorists; and so on?

For example, General David Petraeus was sentenced to 2 years parole and fined $40 thousand dollars for giving classified material to his girlfriend and biographer. It pretty much ruined his career because he swore on his outgoing paperwork from the CIA that he had returned or destroyed all classified material. He obviously didn't! (This may be a bad one.)

Then there is Hillary Clinton. I don't have enough room to mention all of her "issues," so let's just go over the relevant ones. First and foremost, Hillary had ALL her State Department

emails going to her personal server. Illegal, period. Then, she didn't delete the Top Secret and Classified emails from her server after she left or even have it wiped with a "Government safety" level. Again, illegal.

Hillary basically did the same thing the General did. He didn't shred paper copies after he left and she didn't shred electronic copies after she left. He had a small notebook full in his desk drawer, in his house, accessible to only him and people who could get in the house. She has them on her server, attached to the internet, open door to the world, with "home use" security levels. Both the CIA and FBI believe the server was "hacked" by both the Russian and Chinese governments. Don't you feel safe?

RAMBLINGS

Most Democrats say General Petraeus got what he deserved, but maintain that Hillary did nothing wrong! Is it in the DNA?

The General took responsibility. Mrs. Clinton has changed her story several times. Remember, her story went from... it didn't happen, to, she used two phones and got confused, to, she used it but not for secret communications, well, maybe some that weren't marked secret, to, she didn't tell her staff to remove the secret markings but they somehow did, to, Chelsea wiped our server in a post partem moment, to, lie lie lie lie lie lie lie. But you guys on the hard Left see nothing wrong with that and the General was guilty.

The FBI, a very non-partisan organization, came out with the evidence against Hillary and yet somehow there is still no formal charges brought. How does that happen?

As I went through the list of many legislators who were caught in the act (whatever that act is, from playing with interns to taking money to lying under oath) you were more willing to overlook the transgressions of a progressive Democrat than a moderate or conservative Republican. "Equality for all"... sure, that's it.

We have changed our conversation from lie to "misspeak." You know that whole "if you like your doctor you can keep your doctor?" How about Mrs. Clinton dodging bullets at the airport until she saw the video that there wasn't a bullet in the sky and she said she "mis-remembered?" And the whole "hands up don't shoot," but then the black Attorney General and his team investigated to find out it was not true. No apology from the Left for all the accusations.

Many Americans simply see this as an American political pastime. Politicians lie, cheat, and steal. They make up the narrative to suit the situation. Politicians need to justify their existence so you vote them back in. If that requires a little truth bending then so be it! Why?

America, it's our fault! We gave up holding them accountable to the truth. Not my truth, not your truth, but the absolute truth.

If the General signed documents attesting to the fact that he had returned and destroyed all classified papers and didn't do it, then he is guilty. He should have verified before he signed anything. That man had served a life of honor with integrity. We cut him no slack.

~ ~

Many of you on the Left think she is perfect for the job. Apparently you find dishonest people are perfectly suited to run the government.

~ ~

The former Secretary of State knew she didn't destroy the documents and signed that she did. When she "found out" she might have been mistaken, instead of owning up to it, she tried to cover it up and lie about it, like she has done her entire life.

Many of you on the Left think she is perfect for the job. So apparently you find dishonest people are perfectly suited to run the government. You keep doing it and it's worked out so well for you... in Flint, Detroit, Chicago, New Orleans, Baltimore, DC, and Chicago...

Thanks, but no thanks!

When this book went to publish, the FBI recommended NO charges for Hillary, even though the FBI Director stated that she did many things wrong and MAY not have told the truth about some of the issues. No prosecutor would take on this case. Congress has since asked for, and the FBI is conducting, an investigation into her lies to both Congress and the FBI while under oath. As if that weren't enough... another 15,000 emails have been uncovered (and probably won't be the last!).

And the lies just keep on coming!

Chapter 30

It's Over... It's Just Sooooo Over!

Mr. Trump has won. Donald Trump will be the 45th President of these United States. That makes some people cringe and others smile.

America, we had lost our way. We had become exactly what our founding fathers didn't want us to become, a country that was run by the government rather than the people.

Progressiveness scares me. Not the kind that moves us from candles to light bulbs or from horses to cars or from trains to planes. But the kind that says, "We know better than you. Now sit down, be quiet, and let us govern." The kind that says, "We know how much water should flow out of your shower heads. We know how much soda you should drink. We know what kind of food your kids should eat for lunch. We know what's better for you. So shut up, sit down, and let us take care of you."

Hmmmmm. Interesting. Socialist and Communist governments do that. They tell the people what to eat, where to work, how much toilet paper you can have, and so on. We are a representative form of government, NOT a dictatorship. We're not even a "democratic" form of rule in its purest sense.

I know how some people feel. I felt the same way within a year after President Obama took office and then again the second time he won. I felt despair. If it wasn't for the fact that I know who I am in Christ, I might have been doing what some of the rioters did. Not the violence part of it, but the crying and protesting.

Watching Liberal pundits and many in the Democrat party discuss why they lost the 2016 presidency is proof positive that they still have not learned their lesson. Former President Bill Clinton hit the nail on the head, twice, in this campaign and got laughed at. During one speech stumping for his wife, he stated that Obamacare was "a disaster!" The next day, after being sufficiently beaten up, he came out to "clarify" his remarks. Another time he told Hillary's campaign that she needed to go to states like Wisconsin where the average worker was, and he told them not to forget it. They laughed at him on both counts. Who's laughing now?

The Dems forgot about the 99%. PERIOD! The numbers show it. More blue-collar workers voted for the Republican candidate than in past recent elections. It was the same with blacks, Latinos, and Asians. Mrs. Clinton and others would like you to believe that it was the FBI's fault and all the misinformation. Polls show otherwise. The numbers that the different groups voted by show they felt abandoned and lied to. Democrats have forgotten it's a government BY the people, not a government OVER the people.

Democrats have been the Party of entitlement, and I'm not talking about social programs. I'm talking about their politicians. We heard about the "Blue Wall" all during the election. These were supposed to be Democrat strongholds. Most of the solid blue states were ignored by the Party until polls started shifting.

~ ~

When the Democrat party tried to take God out of their platform... it was a sign as to where they were going.

~ ~

Let's get something straight, this was not a vote for Republicans as much as it was a vote for a tear down and rebuild of Washington, D.C. Trump is not seen as a hardcore Republican by Republicans. Yet he is seen as a Right-wing, Republican whack by the media and the Democrat Party. He's sort of a man without a Party. And I, for one, am OK with that!

The country is in need of a major overhaul. For those of you who say the people who voted for Donald Trump are nothing more than Islamophobic, xenophobic, racist, bigot, woman-haters, you are nothing more than ignorant political hacks with no understanding of America. And for those of you who called those of us who didn't vote for Mr. Obama (TWICE!) racist are also ignorant of American values.

RAMBLINGS

Most of us who didn't vote for Obama knew he wouldn't do a good job. Period. Those of us who didn't vote for Hillary knew she was the poster child for corruption.

America has done a lot wrong in its years of finding itself. I'm not listing any of them here. Do your own homework. But the U.S. has done much good around the world providing humanitarian aid, financial aid, protecting countries who ask for our help, getting people out of harm's way, bringing medical help when needed, and so much more. NO OTHER COUNTRY has stepped up more often with more resources to help non-Americans that the Unites Stated of America.

Are we perfect? NO! Are we getting better? YES! Every day, every week, every year we become a better society, a better people, and a better world neighbor.

The era of the Democrats ruling over the poor and minorities is over. Minorities got the message and has seen what over 50 years of Democrat rule has done to them... and they're tired of it. Democrats have moved too far to the Left not paying attention to Middle America.

Republicans have scared the crap out of many in America with their hardcore, in-your-face Conservative values. Don't get me wrong, I LOVE Conservative values, but I am not most people in America. The age of Progressive Republicanism is making its way into the Party and will eventually clash hard with true Conservatives. I don't know what that will do. My crystal ball stopped working years ago.

When the Democrat party tried to take God out of their platform and then repented, it was a sign as to where they were going. When they left out the American flags at the convention, it was another sign. And when they left Jesus out of their prayers at the DNC it too was a sign, "Cliff Ahead."

Democrats have forgotten the average America. And they have forgotten that you can only push and squeeze people so long and so hard before they rebel.

It's sooooo over. Politics in America will never be the same. Thank you God for having a hand in this shakeup. Thank you to my fellow evangelicals who saw the signs and came out and voted at 82% for

It's Over... It's Just Sooooo Over!

Donald Trump for a fighting chance to keep our religious liberties. Thank you to the many Democrats who finally saw the light and recognized their own Party telling them they were too stupid and ignorant to be self-sufficient and make it on their own, without a nanny government. Thanks to the Average American who was tired of the political cesspool in Washington, D.C. and said enough.

Can Republicans fix it? I have no clue. But they govern different than Democrats who have had control for many years.

Now is the time to have Hope and pray for Change.

Chapter 31

One Last Ramble...

It's my first book and frankly I could have easy rambled on for dozens and dozens of chapters. Like many of you, I'm tired of hearing about white privilege, trigger warnings, safe rooms, not inclusive enough, too gender specific, and the rest of the list of politically correct garbage that could fill another 100 pages!

Listeners often email me saying they've never heard about any of this craziness. I used to ask why but then realized that most of them are working, yep, trying to keep food on the table and a roof over their heads. They can't scan the entire interweb or cable or social media. They rely on people like me and others that they trust to put it out there and inform them.

For the first time in my adult life, I am concerned for the welfare of this country. We accept lying as a way of life. Responsibility is a thing of the past, and honor and integrity are old-fashioned ideals only your grandma and grandpa think about.

America, I'm here to tell you that we can win it back. Stop allowing it to happen. Stop listening to those that make you feel bad about being white or having morals or believing in God or that there is a right and wrong. Those principles are what made this country great.

We knew who we were. We knew we were Americans, part of the greatest nation on this planet. The great things we have accomplished far outweigh the mistakes we have made and the proof of our greatness is our continued drive to fix those mistakes and make them right.

We have tried so hard to make a better life for the next generation that I fear we have actually harmed them. By not pushing them to do better, be better, try harder, push through, and be the best you can be, we have done them a great injustice.

One Last Ramble...

We have raised a group of "people" who can't handle any ill feelings. They need counseling if they hear or see anything that offends them, and actually want guarantees that they won't be offended or hurt them in any way, not only on campus BUT in life!

Can you imagine if the "greatest generation" this country has known had refused to fight Hitler or the Japanese because bombing others made them feel bad? Or that fighting to secure country borders is not right? Or that religious rights aren't worth defending? Maybe if we just let the enemy know we loved them and wanted to give them hugs (cue the Kumbaya song). What did my generation do to screw things up so bad?

Shame on us for not instilling patriotism in our children, respect for authority, and an understanding that there were people and causes out there that were much more important than them.

It's not too late. We can win it all back. Keep speaking to your children, grandchildren, niece, nephews, and people you work with.

Take the chance our forefathers did. Those who fought in the Civil War, brother against brother, to make the wrong of slavery right. They never gave up. Against the entire British Army, they never gave up. Against mounting casualties, bad weather, and little resources... they never gave up.

Americans never give up. We can win! At least that's this one right-wing, Bible-thumping, white man's rambling opinion!

Acknowledgments

Jesus Christ *My Lord and savior and whom I would be nothing without. (You should get to know Him!)*

Tammy Messina *Wife, mother, producer, "Help mate," lover of Christ, poker and prodder of Joe. Favorite line "You really want to do this Joe?"*

Rick Green *Probably one of my biggest influences. Loves God, family and country. He lives it without apology and without ceasing. His energy and genuine love for them inspired me to "turn it up!"*

Sonja Schmidt *Pounded me about proper English grammar and titles! Hmmmm, almost like a second wife!*

Dr. Gina Loudon *Pushed me from **day one** to be true to myself and not give in to the pressure I was going to get from station owners and others!*

Evan Sayet *Taught me nothing is sacred... Don't be PC... Don't be a bully, but be passionate and use facts!*

Tim Maranville *FIRST syndicator who gave me a chance. First person willing to let me know when he thought I was off and what made my show special!*

Sandy Frazier *My PR and booking person. Always encouraging me to write (I hate writing) and keep writing with passion and sarcasm as a way to get the message across.*

A.F. Branco *For generously sharing his talent of putting more than a thousand words into each political cartoon to drive the points home!*

My Big Italian family... *"Spirited" conversations around the dinner table, fluctuating volumes to get our points across or to be heard. I learned how to keep my finger on several conversations and issues at the same time and to respect each other's viewpoints, UNLESS it directly hurt family and then... Well, use your imagination!*

AND if I left anyone out, it wasn't intentional. There's only so much space!

About the Author

Every day loyal listeners spanning the entire United States and 38 countries tune in to hear current news stories that are rarely heard through other news outlets. Why?

You know all those topics that no one wants to talk about? And old, white guys *definitely* aren't supposed to talk about? Well, that's Joe's comfort zone! Yes, all those politically incorrect topics... every social issue, religion, LGBTQ (yes, there's a Q... and MORE!), abortion, traditional family, gay marriage, education, the war on women, the war on religion, the war on Christianity (and pretty much any other war that the Left wants to fabricate!) and, of course, politics.

Joe Messina is decidedly conservative and an outspoken Bible-believing, Christian. Yet his guests will tell you, the conversation is always respectful, even when they're on completely different sides of the issue. For Joe, it's all about having the conversation so that you know what "the other side" thinks.

Practicing what he preaches, Joe is actively engaged in his local community and church, and is very involved in politics. Having the reputation of being a man of integrity and ethics, he is

regularly asked to teach business ethics for various organizations.

Joe's goal for the show (and now a book!)... Make sure that anyone listening can understand the conversation and walk away with new and useful information using clear simple English. No political speak. No double talk. Just REAL facts... REAL words... REAL conversation.

Stop by and say hello at: **www.TheRealSide.com**